Interviewing for Journalists

Interviewing for Journalists details the central journalistic skill of how to ask the right question in the right way. It is a practical and concise guide for all print and online journalists – professionals, students and trainees – whether writing news stories or features for newspapers and magazines, print or web pages.

Interviewing for Journalists focuses on the many types of interviewing, from the vox pop and press conference to the interview used as the basis of an in-depth profile. Featuring interviews with a number of successful journalists such as Emma Brockes of the *Guardian* and *New York Times* and Andrew Duncan of *Radio Times*, *Interviewing for Journalists* covers every stage of interviews including research, planning and preparation, structuring questions, the vital importance of body language, how to get a vivid quote, checking and editing material and suiting questions to face-to-face and web interviews.

Interviewing for Journalists includes:

- discussion of the importance of the interview for journalism
- advice on how to handle different interviewees such as politicians, celebrities and vulnerable people
- how to carry out web, telephone and face-to-face interviews
- hints on note-taking, shorthand and recording methods for both print and on-line interviews
- discussion of ethical, legal and professional issues such as libel, privacy, cheque-book journalism, off-the-record briefings and the limits of editing
- a glossary of journalistic terms and notes on further reading.

Sally Adams is a freelance journalist. She wrote the feature section of *Writing for Journalists*.

Wynford Hicks is a freelance journalist and editorial trainer. He is the author of *English for Journalists*, now in its third edition, and *Writing for Journalists*, now in its second edition.

Media Skills

EDITED BY: RICHARD KEEBLE, LINCOLN UNIVERSITY
SERIES ADVISERS: WYNFORD HICKS AND JENNY MCKAY

The *Media Skills* series provides a concise and thorough introduction to a rapidly changing media landscape. Each book is written by media and journalism lecturers or experienced professionals and is a key resource for a particular industry. Offering helpful advice and information and using practical examples from print, broadcast and digital media, as well as discussing ethical and regulatory issues, *Media Skills* books are essential guides for students and media professionals.

English for Journalists
3rd edition
Wynford Hicks

Writing for Journalists
2nd edition
Wynford Hicks with Sally Adams, Harriett Gilbert and Tim Holmes

Interviewing for Radio
Jim Beaman

Web Production for Writers and Journalists
2nd edition
Jason Whittaker

Ethics for Journalists
2nd edition
Richard Keeble

Scriptwriting for the Screen
2nd edition
Charlie Moritz

Interviewing for Journalists
Sally Adams, with Wynford Hicks

Researching for Television and Radio
Adèle Emm

Reporting for Journalists
Chris Frost

Subediting for Journalists
Wynford Hicks and Tim Holmes

Designing for Newspapers and Magazines
Chris Frost

Writing for Broadcast Journalists
Rick Thompson

Freelancing for Television and Radio
Leslie Mitchell

Programme Making for Radio
Jim Beaman

Magazine Production
Jason Whittaker

Production Management for Television
Leslie Mitchell

Feature Writing for Journalists
Sharon Wheeler

Find more details of current *Media Skills* books and forthcoming titles at www.producing.routledge.com

Interviewing for Journalists

Second Edition

Sally Adams
with Wynford Hicks

LONDON AND NEW YORK

First published 2001
by Routledge
2 Park Square, Milton Park, Abingdon, Oxon OX14 4RN

Simultaneously published in the USA and Canada
by Routledge
711 Third Avenue, New York, NY 10017

This edition published 2009

Routledge is an imprint of the Taylor & Francis Group, an informa business

Typeset in Goudy and Scala Sans by
Florence Production Ltd, Stoodleigh, Devon
Printed and bound in Great Britain by
CPI Antony Rowe, Chippenham, Wiltshire

British Library Cataloguing in Publication Data
A catalogue record for this book is available from the British Library

Library of Congress Cataloging in Publication Data
Adams, Sally, 1933–.
Interviewing for journalists/Sally Adams with Wynford Hicks.
– 2nd ed.
p. cm. – (Media skills)
Includes bibliographical references and index.
1. Interviewing in journalism. I. Hicks, Wynford, 1942–.
II. Title.
PN4784.I6A33 2009
070.4′3 – dc22 2008041925

ISBN10: 0–415–47774–3 (hbk)
ISBN10: 0–415–47775–1 (pbk)
ISBN10: 0–203–88885–5 (ebk)

ISBN13: 978–0–415–47774–1 (hbk)
ISBN13: 978–0–415–47775–8 (pbk)
ISBN13: 978–0–203–88885–8 (ebk)

Contents

Contributors

Sally Adams is a freelance journalist and writer. She has worked as deputy editor of *She*, editor of *Mother and Baby* and *Weight Watchers Magazine*, as a reporter on the *Christchurch Press*, New Zealand and as the letters page editor on the *San Francisco Chronicle*. She has written for the *Guardian*, *Daily Mail*, *Company*, *Evening Standard*, *Good Housekeeping*, and wrote the 'Feature' section of *Writing for Journalists*, now in its second edition.

Wynford Hicks has worked as a reporter, subeditor, feature writer, editor and editorial consultant for newspapers, books and magazines and as a teacher of journalism specialising in writing, subediting and the use of English. He is the author of various books on journalism and writing, including *English for Journalists*, now in its third edition, *Writing for Journalists* and *Quite Literally: Problem Words and How to Use Them*.

Brendan Martin is a journalist of more than 30 years' experience of newspapers, magazines and radio. He has also worked as a journalism trainer and lecturer since 1994. He has written for *The Times*, *Daily Express*, *Daily Mail*, *TVTimes*, *Radio Times* and *Woman's Own*. He is Visiting Lecturer at City University, London, and Associate Lecturer at the London College of Communication.

Emma Lee-Potter is a freelance journalist and editor. She trained with Mirror Group Newspapers and later worked as a staff news reporter for the *Evening Standard*, *Sunday Express* and *Today*. She now writes for the *Guardian*, *Daily Express*, *Mail on Sunday* and *New Statesman*, and is the author of four novels.

Amber Tokeley is a freelance journalist and former editor of *Home & Country* magazine. She has written for a range of titles including *Company*, *Home*, *Weight Watchers*, the *Sydney Morning Herald*, *Cleo* (Australia's answer to *Company*), and has contributed to several non-fiction books.

1
Introduction
Wynford Hicks

Interviewing is the central activity in modern journalism. It is the main means by which reporters and feature writers gather their material.

According to Christopher Silvester,[1] the interview came to Britain from the United States towards the end of the nineteenth century. It was part of the 'new journalism' that turned the media world upside down. From a stuffy, pompous thing that could interest only a minority of the serious-minded, journalism became a lively means of informing and entertaining millions of people.

As journalism developed, interviewing became increasingly important. The journalist as observer and recorder, attending a political meeting to report the leader's speech in detail or describing, shell by shell, daily life in a town under fire or joining the mourners at a gangster's funeral, still exists, of course. But reporting is incomplete without interviews: readers want to know how bystanders, eye-witnesses, participants reacted to what happened, what they thought and felt about it.

Even in sport the match report is followed by the post-match interview – and that's once a week. On the other six days the interview – with the sport star, the star's manager, the star's partner or one-night stand, the star's hairdresser – dominates. And let's not forget the sport star's 'column', based on an interview by a journalist on the sports desk.

In every area of newspaper and magazine coverage the interview is a way of bringing human interest into stories. It helps satisfy that powerful curiosity about the lives of the famous. But, much more than that, it is the means by which the journalist goes about gathering material. Interviews with experts and prominent people add credibility and authority to copy. Interviews with those involved in a news event – an eye-witness to an accident or a surviving victim – take a story beyond the reporter's necessarily restricted view.

In the Anglo-American tradition, interviewing sources and attributing facts and opinions to them is an essential part of reporting. Indeed, in many newspapers, otherwise sound stories that can't be supported by quotes remain unpublished.

And interviews can make news. A person who has publishable information can use an interview to reveal it at a time of their own choosing, perhaps promising the journalist an exclusive to try to ensure the kind of exposure they want. Or an enterprising reporter can track down a person they know or suspect has important information. The resulting interview then becomes the story.

The interview can be defined as a prearranged face-to-face meeting between a journalist, who asks questions, and an interviewee, who answers them. The interviewee is often notable (or notorious) and the questions usually focus on them, their life and their opinions. But this book also uses the wider definition that applies to all journalists who write news or features. Here, interviewing is asking people questions to gather material for publication, both information and quotes.

So an interview may consist of a quick phone call to check a fact or an afternoon spent recording someone's life story. But brief or elaborate, a phone call or a face-to-face meeting, the successful interview comes from a professional approach. And it is the purpose of this book to explain and illustrate that approach, giving practical advice.

The book is based on the author's experience gained in many years of interviewing for a variety of newspapers and magazines, and on a series of interviews with other journalists conducted for the book. Some of these are well known; others less so; others again have chosen not to be named.

One consequence of asking practitioners how they work (as opposed to pontificating from the outside) is that there are occasionally differences of emphasis in their replies. More noticeable, though, is how much agreement there is on the essentials of interviewing: prepare thoroughly, listen carefully, edit accurately, and so on.

Interviewing for Journalists concentrates on print. But it is impossible to ignore the influence of broadcasting. For example, everybody who has heard John Humphrys and seen Jeremy Paxman in action will be familiar with the confrontational interview. On the positive side, interviewees now expect tough questioning when this is appropriate. But on the negative side trainee print journalists may be tempted to copy the Humphrys–Paxman approach – and needlessly antagonise their interviewees.

Another powerful influence on the print interview is the increasing ease and acceptability of recording. A digital recorder enables the interviewer to concentrate on what the interviewee is actually saying, keeping eye contact. But, on the downside, transcription can take a long time and the printed interview, if not well edited, can be wordy and repetitive.

It's a truism that this is a media-conscious age: media studies courses abound and there is some (though not enough) practical journalism training. And just as journalism students and trainee journalists practise interviewing, their counterparts go on media-awareness courses and practise being interviewed. If anything confirms the need for good, thorough journalism training, it's the inclusion of interview techniques and news management skills in corporate training schemes.

The core of this book is the prearranged set-piece interview, which is discussed in stages from research and planning to checking and editing quotes. (Writing techniques as such are not covered in this book but in another in the series, *Writing for Journalists*.)

This edition includes a new chapter by Brendan Martin of City University on interviewing for the internet. Other chapters cover note-taking and recording, and approaches to different kinds of interviewees: politicians; celebrities; and special cases, such as the reluctant and inexperienced, business people, the vulnerable, children and the bereaved, the PR sitting in on the interview, and interviewers doubling up.

But this section does not claim to be comprehensive. For example, although the book includes references to the investigative journalist, it does not attempt to give advice on how to work undercover, how to lay traps for corrupt politicians, etc.

Various issues – ethical, legal, professional – raised by the practice of interviewing are discussed as they arise. These points are brought together in the final chapter – a chapter which was particularly hard to write. It is one thing to lay down general principles and draft codes of practice – especially for other people to follow. It is much harder to decide what to do in specific situations. So, if there is a lack of certainty in some of the advice offered, it is because, ultimately, you the journalist must find your own answers to the questions raised.

Note

1 C. Silvester, *The Penguin Book of Interviews: An Anthology from 1859 to the Present Day*, Viking, 1993.

2 Basics of communicating and interviewing

Skilled journalists make interviewing look easy. They quickly get on their interviewee's wavelength and encourage them to talk freely. They ask questions that elicit lively replies, listen to what's said, note what they hear while thinking of the next question, at the same time checking what they've just heard against what they know from research.

They cajole answers from the reluctant, corral the waffly, reassure the nervous, recognise fudges, check ambiguities – and all within a set time while talking to someone they've probably never met before. They make it look easy but it isn't. If journalism is a craft, interviewing is an art. There are a lot of unrelated skills to master and, like learning to drive a car, interviewing is daunting and difficult at first. But, with practice, setting off smoothly, signalling, changing gear, steering and watching the instruments become second nature. So it is with interviewing.

The most useful characteristic for an all-round interviewer is to be likeable, the sort of person who can get on with almost anybody and is interested in everybody: a person who people are happy to talk to, who comes across as a human being first, a journalist second.

The most valuable attribute is probably curiosity, followed by charm, keen powers of observation, doggedness, flexibility and fairness. Then add the ability to think fast, analyse, keep a poker face when necessary, a broad general knowledge and plenty of scepticism . . .

It's a rare journalist who can master the complete range of styles that interviewing demands. A brilliant fact-extractor is unlikely to produce a good interview with an unhappy transsexual for *Marie Claire*, just as a sympathetic and understanding feature specialist probably wouldn't produce a good interview with the chancellor of the exchequer for *Investors' Chronicle*. Each type of interview requires a different approach. Then, to add to the complications, there are the abrasions of personality to consider. This is why self-effacing interviewers can be so successful, like the 'invisible' photographer who people forget is there.

Interviewing is also a skill best mastered progressively. There's a certain order to it, as there is in life. Just as children crawl before they walk, walk before they run and run before they play football – so it is with interviewing.

So, if you want to become a good all-round interviewer, please start here. Skipping the basics is the equivalent of hitting the ground running with zero practice.

First, it's important to realise what the interviewer–interviewee relationship entails. You will use people, and you will be used. You will find some people who divulge little, others who tell you more than you wish to know. You will be trusted with secrets, you will be lied to. You will be bombarded with what seem like irrelevancies and only later realise what a key piece one of them is in the information jigsaw. You will be rebuffed, you will be courted.

As a result of what you write, based on what you learn during an interview, people may lose their jobs, companies may close, lives may be ruined. Or you may be intrigued enough to try out a new sport, meet someone you later marry, win an award.

Some interviewees may have second thoughts. They may ask you to pretty-up or sanitise their words. They may beg you not to print what they said, and some may use threats. These decisions usually rest with the editor, but a time may come when you are the one who has to decide. Journalists who have been interviewed and regret what they have said, or fear they will be misrepresented, will understand. A former *Mirror* writer involved in a shares scandal said after he'd been sacked: 'I've written some pretty nasty things about people but when it's done to you it's bloody awful.' For most journalists, the first time someone pleads with them to alter copy is when the real power of the press hits home.

Editorial policy

Let's assume, first, that you are working for a publication that has an editorial policy, that is, it knows what it is trying to achieve and why. This should describe realistically how the publication intends to reach its readers – for example, by informing and/or amusing them, by helping or persuading them. Editorial policies are important because, if you don't know what you are trying to achieve, you're flailing round in a fog.

Let's assume, second, that you work for a publication that knows a lot about its readers and understands how to interest them. And third, that it's a publication where you're regularly sent out to get stories face-to-face as well as on the telephone.

Here, alas, we're talking about an ideal. All too often in newspaper and magazine offices the emphasis is on productivity and speed. Reporters now mostly interview over the phone, and going out on a story can be seen as a luxury. Wrong: look on it as a necessity. It may be worth reminding your news editor of what they already know: that face-to-face interviews produce better stories. You benefit too: get it right face-to-face and you learn *all* the interviewing skills. Do it solely on the telephone and your repertoire will be incomplete.

There are reporters now on local papers who have to produce five, six, seven and even more news stories a day. Nick Davies, author of *Flat Earth News*, describes journalists who have to write huge numbers of news stories as being 'chained to a keyboard on a production line in a news factory, churning out trivia and cliché; to fill space in the paper'. Not pleasant, not satisfying, not a good idea – but a reality that must be faced.

Communication

One more necessity. We can't start until we have looked at the maze that is communication. When two people communicate, a lot can go wrong in a very short time. Say we call a (male) interviewer A and a (female) interviewee B. In a simple question and answer exchange you have to take into account the following:

- What A thinks he says.
- What A actually says.

- What B thinks she hears.
- What B actually hears.
- What B actually says in reply.
- What A thinks he hears B say.

A is interviewing B about arguments at work. B is talking about a row at a previous job.

- B ends by saying: 'So I left.'
- B thinks she has said: 'I left work early that day.'
- A thinks he hears: 'So I quit my job.'
- A says: 'Did you regret the decision?'
- B thinks: 'What a stupid question.'
- B says: 'No.'
- A thinks B is glad she left her previous job and is happy in her present one, which may or may not be true.

Add to this the many more mistakes that can happen during a telephone interview, where the interviewer is unable to see reactions.

Or:

- A is interviewing B on the phone about experiences as an adult education teacher and asks: 'How do you get on with the old?'
- B hears real insensitivity: 'the old', not 'older people'. Starts to go off A immediately.
- B replies: 'Older people are exceptionally rewarding to teach.'
- A agrees enthusiastically, thinking about teaching IT to 80 year olds: 'Yes, aren't they – the old have got so much to learn.' A thinks that sounds understanding.
- B sees it as showing that A thinks older people are stupid.

This applies at all levels. Alan Greenspan, one-time chairman of the US government's powerful Federal Reserve Bank, is on record as telling Wall Street economists: 'I know you believe you understand what you think I said but I am not sure you realise that what you heard is not what I meant.'

The best way to avoid misunderstanding is to use feedback: if at all uncertain, repeat back to your interviewee what you believe they said. This doesn't mean you need to paraphrase every word slowly and clearly, enunciating distinctly, but rather that you recognise accuracy to be in both your interests and that there are many factors which can cause mistakes. These include – for both of you – stress, prejudice, tiredness, distraction, a closed mind.

Back to the start ...

Before you begin planning interviews, there is one important rite of passage to undergo: you must learn to sniff out news. The approach is quite simple: jump right in at the deep end. It's not easy for beginners. In fact it can be downright difficult and embarrassing, but it happens to the best, and once you're out and on the other side, you're on your way.

Andrew Marr, formerly political editor of the BBC, started his career as a reporter on a daily paper. A training course went with the job, and he remembers it vividly. 'We were sent off to local villages and outlying suburbs ... and told not to come back until we had half a dozen publishable stories ... That meant slowly scrubbing away any natural shyness, banging on vicars' doors, stopping shopkeepers and pleading with councillors for anything – anything. Stray dog? Upset at the Guild? Oldest villager?'

By the time the six stories were written, not only had the trainees learned what makes a news story but any reluctance about interviewing had disappeared. Many journalists are shy at first, but the urge or necessity to find stories is so strong that they become interviewers despite themselves.

Not everybody finds that recognising a good story comes easily. My favourite anecdote, supposedly true, is about a trainee who was sent off to get a story from a women's football club but came back disheartened. 'No luck,' he said. 'They're not playing. They're all pregnant.'

Along with learning to recognise publishable stories goes the necessity to be accurate, and that includes spelling names correctly and not – please not – mangling the English language. Never forget that the people you are working for, particularly the news editor, feature editors and – that annoyingly knowledgeable group – the subs, spend their days working with, and respecting, the English language. Rotten spelling, gruesome punctuation and ghastly grammar exasperate them.

Australian journalist Phillip Knightley remembers how he learned to be accurate when he started his first job as a reporter in New South Wales, where the idea of interviewing someone on the telephone never occurred to them. They went out and met people face-to-face. They were part of the community.

> We knew everybody and everybody knew us. If I got someone's second initial wrong, they would stop me on the street to complain. If I got the whole story wrong, I would never hear the end of it.
>
> The *Northern Star* taught me to be accurate, that people had feelings and that you could not use your privileged access as a journalist to come into their lives, suck them dry and then leave them. You had personal and civic responsibilities.

The foundation stones

Once the requirements of news stories are mastered, the business of interview planning can begin. So here's a quick whizz-round to give you an idea of the whole interviewing process.

The simplest task is collecting information, which is why beginners are often sent off to cover garden shows or weddings and funerals, which all require collecting a lot of names and where the questions are relatively simple. Correct spelling can't be overemphasised. As one news editor said memorably, though unkindly, about his readers: 'The bastards may not be able to read or write but they know how to spell their own names.'

Accuracy also applies to the names of roads, streets, villages and towns wherever they are, though some Scottish, Welsh and Irish names can be particularly complex. For example, the Scottish town whose name is pronounced Pennycook is written Penicuik; another is pronounced Hoyck but written Hawick. For *all* names, unless you know them *for certain*, check the spelling.

For names you don't know at all, check letter by letter, using capital letters if you're using a notebook. Is it Nixon, Nikkson, Nixone, Nickson? Is it Mackenzie, Makenzie, Mackensie? John, Jon, Jonn? Naturally, if you're collecting the names of business people, wherever possible get hold of their cards. Remember, too, that in Chinese the family name goes first. Our 'first name' comes second with them.

Next come more complicated news stories, all requiring extra planning. Everything used in mastering news stories provides the basis on which features rest, and they enjoy almost boundless freedom in structure, content, approach and variety, developing from very simple features to complex interviews with politicians and celebrities.

Time to begin.

News interviewing

The basics

Modern technology has transformed newspaper and magazine production beyond recognition in the last 20 years, but when it comes to writing a news story, the basic Who? What? When? Where? Why? How? questions remain as essential as ever. Keep these six in mind on every news story you cover and you'll find it much easier to write your copy afterwards.

For instance, if you are covering a planning row for a weekly newspaper, you'll need to know:

- **Who** are the individuals, company or organisation seeking planning permission, and who are those protesting against it?
- **What** does the planning application entail? Is it a school, shopping centre, luxury block of flats?
- **When** are the key dates? When was the application submitted, for example, and when is the next meeting to discuss it?
- **Where** is the proposed development?
- **Why** are protesters so unhappy about it? Why do supporters think it should go ahead? You will need to speak to representatives from both sides to report their views.
- **How** are protesters planning to show their disapproval? How are supporters hoping to convince the community that the planning application should go ahead?

If you are covering a burglary for an evening newspaper you'll need to ask:

- **Who** was the victim of the burglary? Was it an individual or a business? Were they of particular note in the area your newspaper covers? Are they offering a reward?

- **What** was stolen (items and their worth)?
- **When** did the burglary take place?
- **Where** did the burglary take place?
- **Why** did the burglary take place? Was the burgled property in a wealthy area, for example?
- **How** did the burglary occur? It's important to ask what, if any, security measures were in place and where the owners/employers were at the time. Did the intruder smash a window to get in, pick a lock or elude an alarm system?

There will, of course, be many other questions to ask along the way, but getting the basic details in your notebook is absolutely key.

Techniques to remember

Whether you are interviewing face-to-face or on the telephone, it's important to concentrate on the way you introduce yourself and launch into the interview. You should:

- Approach people confidently.
- Give your name and the name of the publication you work for.
- Ask clear questions.
- Listen to the answers.
- Recognise a good story when you see one.
- Encourage the interviewee to keep talking.
- Extract lively quotes.

If you can do all these things, along with getting the details right, keeping to your deadline and writing a simple, uncluttered intro, then you'll be on course to producing good news stories.

How to prepare

Before you interview anyone, whether in person or on the phone, you must:

- **Plan.** Work out in advance what you need and want to know. Plan your questions and the topics you want to cover.
- **Research.** Before you meet your interviewee, try to find out as much as you possibly can about them. Read previous interviews,

trawl the internet for information and talk to other people who have met them. There may be little information available or you may be very tight for time, but recognise that being prepared will give you the edge – particularly when it comes to business, political and celebrity interviews.

- **Be punctual.** Make sure you arrive in good time for the interview. Arriving late will irritate your interviewee and you'll have lost valuable interviewing time.

The interview itself

During the interview you should:

- **Listen.** Once the interview has started, no matter how tempted you are, don't talk about yourself or deviate from the purpose of the interview. Silence really is golden.
- **Empathise.** This doesn't mean that you have to like your interviewee, but that you think yourself into their skin and are aware of the likely impact of your questions.

These key principles – plan, research, listen, empathise – underpin successful interviews. You should also:

- Always tell your interviewee who you are, right at the outset. Give your name and the publication you are working for.

- Fit in. Dress in a way that suits your interviewee and the occasion. Use language they feel comfortable with.

- Ensure you have all the basic details. For local newspapers these will include name, age, occupation and address. Always check spellings, no matter how obvious a name may seem. For specialist magazines, a person's age may be irrelevant so the basic details will be different. For a business title, 'must-knows' will probably include job title, company turnover and number of employees, while for a slimming magazine it might be a person's weight and weight lost.

- Listen and record (by notebook, recorder or both). Don't argue, judge or show embarrassment. Ask questions in a logical order. If your questions jump about it will confuse your interviewee and may interrupt the flow of the interview. But then again, don't stick to your list of questions so rigidly that you miss an unexpected follow-up question, new revelation or angle.

- Recognise that vivid quotes are the key to a great interview. Ask effective questions – questions that elicit lively replies – rather than a series of closed 'yes' and 'no' answers. 'Making the first million is hard, making the next 100 million is easy,' businessman Theo Paphitis told *Daily Telegraph* writer Celia Walden. A great quote; it wouldn't have been half so interesting if he'd said 'It was more difficult when I started out than it is now.' Keep the interviewing moving with responsive questions. 'Really?' 'What happened next?'
- Don't rush to fill the gaps in conversation. 'Interviewees often appreciate a bit of time and space to think about what they want to say,' says freelance writer Emma Lee-Potter. 'One of the first stories I covered as a trainee reporter was a golden wedding, and every time the elderly couple stopped talking for a second I asked another question. Arthur Kay, the photographer I worked with, told me not to be scared of silences. He said people often come up with better quotes when they have time to collect their thoughts. And he was absolutely right.'
- Keep an open mind. You might not find the story you were expecting – but then again you might find an even better one.
- Remember all the elements of the story. Where relevant, take notes on your interviewee's appearance, expressions, the room in which interview takes place, etc. Even a photograph or painting on the wall may lead them to something interesting. See page 69.
- At the end of the interview, consider asking: 'Is there anything else you'd like to add?' Works better for business and first-time interviewees. Bear in mind, though, that when journalist Emma Brockes asked broadcaster Clive James a question along these lines he told her: 'I'm not doing your work for you!'
- Think pix. Never forget the picture angle when you're working on a story. If you haven't got a photographer with you, note down the picture possibilities and give contact details to the picture desk.
- Be prepared to learn from your mistakes.

- Be charming and polite – even if you disagree profoundly with the views you're hearing. Be sceptical rather than adversarial.
- It's important, too, to empathise, especially if you are interviewing someone who has been through a traumatic experience. As freelance editor and writer Melanie Whitehouse says: 'Empathy is vital. People think you have to be hard to be a successful journalist, but I believe that, while a tough exterior helps, a soft interior is a must. How else can you ever relate to the woman who is telling you how her daughter was murdered, or that her husband beat her up? You need to develop the ability to win someone's trust in a matter of minutes, and you should not abuse that trust.'
- Finally, never forget that it's the interviewee who's the star.

If you stick to these guidelines, you won't go far wrong. But all interviews are different, in terms of style, substance and length.

Here are some of the types of interview you may be asked to do in the early years of your career.

The 'calls'

Most local newspaper reporters take their turn at doing the 'calls' – phoning the police, fire and ambulance services regularly to check whether they have a story. This is the simplest kind of interviewing and your approach should be clear, businesslike and courteous.

Following up a tip

News desks frequently receive tip-offs about stories. Whether they are tips about muggings, fires or graffiti being scrawled on the town hall's wall, the essence of each story – the who, what, when, where, why and how – will need checking out, either in person or on the phone.

Sometimes these tip-offs won't lead anywhere, but often, particularly in local newspapers, they will produce very worthwhile stories.

CASE STUDY 1

The news desk of an evening newspaper gets a tip-off that a house is on fire in its area. The address is confirmed by a call to the fire service. When you, the reporter, arrive at the scene, the firefighters have left but you spot a neighbour standing in her front garden. What should you ask her?

After introducing yourself and saying a few sympathetic words, the most effective way to start is by asking: 'Please tell me what happened.' Note down what the woman says and, when she has finished, go back to the beginning and ask questions to fill in the gaps.

- Who is the neighbour? Check her name, how it is spelled, her age and what she does for a living. Who lives at the house that was on fire? Were they in the house at the time of the fire, for instance, or out at work? Was anyone killed or injured in the fire? If anyone was injured or trapped, who rescued them?
- What happened? Ask the neighbour to give a first-hand view of what she saw.
- When did the fire start? When did the neighbour realise something was wrong?
- Where exactly was the fire? Your story will need to explain where the house is – street, town, etc. Where in the house did it start?
- Why did it start? It may be too early to ascertain the cause of the fire but the fire service and the neighbour herself may have theories.
- How much damage has the fire caused? How will the fire affect the owners of the property and the local community?

These are the types of question that will help you to build up a vivid, authentic story. You will need to make follow-up calls to the police, fire and ambulance services to check whether anyone has been injured or killed in the fire and to get a fuller account of the incident, as well as speaking to the owners of the house, but the neighbour's description of what she saw will give you a good start to your story.

Make sure you have every possible angle covered. As Bill Browne, former editor of the *Basingstoke Gazette* and now publisher of *Salisbury Journal*, says: 'My biggest mistake as a junior was to think the deadline was so important that you got in and got out as quickly as you could. Now I know that, the longer you stay, the better story you write.

'Milk every job for every last line you can get out of it. Then, when the news editor asks you a question about what you haven't included, you can answer it. Rush away or put the phone down if the deadline demands it, but not if you think that's what journalists do.'

CASE STUDY 2

The news desk of a weekly paper gets a call from a woman in an outlying village complaining about traffic congestion. More and more cars are using the village as a short-cut and she's worried that the extra traffic is proving dangerous for residents and drivers alike. The news editor gives you the woman's address and asks you to check out the story.

The best way to check this story out – time permitting – is to visit the village in person, see the problem for yourself, and interview the woman and her neighbours. You will need to find out:

- Who is unhappy about the traffic congestion? Ask their basic details (e.g. their name, age, job, address, how long they have lived in the village, whether they have any village responsibilities such as sitting on the parish council, etc.).
- What is the essence of their complaint? Are there times of the day when the traffic is particularly bad? Have villagers surveyed the volume of the traffic? Have there been more accidents? What do they intend to do about it (letters, meetings with the county council, etc.)?
- When did the problem start?
- Where is the problem? You will need to name the roads involved.
- Why did the problem start? Is there a particular reason for the congestion, such as the closure of another road or the development of a new industrial estate nearby?
- How are residents planning to show their concern about the congestion? Have they started a petition, for example, or perhaps involved their local MP?

Once you have the answers to these questions, along with some lively quotes from villagers, you will need to get the views of the county council. All county councils have press officers so, unless you have your own contact, ring them and ask to be put in touch with a relevant officer and councillor.

Vox pops

The term comes from the Latin *vox populi* – or 'the voice of the people'. Editors often use vox pops as a cheap and easy way to fill a page with pictures and short quotes from people interviewed in the street about current topics – anything from their views on the economy to the latest 'EastEnders' storyline.

Vox pops are a great way to practise basic interviewing skills. Interviewees are often flattered to be asked for their views, and you learn to get basic details, precise answers and short, snappy quotes. You can also discard any interviews that don't work because the answers were dull or irrelevant.

When embarking on a vox pop, make sure you have a relevant, interesting question to ask. Choose a spot where you're likely to find the journalistic equivalent of a captive audience – people who are waiting for a bus, for instance, or queuing to get into a club. Shopping centres and street markets can also be productive areas. Use your common sense, though. Don't approach people laden with shopping, or parents looking after several small children – especially if the children are playing up.

Walk up to people confidently, notebook and pen in hand. Never use a clipboard – everyone will think you're doing market research. Smile, be positive and use the word 'journalist', along with your name and the publication you're working for, as early as possible.

> 'Hello. I'm a journalist for . . . and I'm writing a feature on . . . What are your views?'
>
> 'Hello, I'm a journalist interviewing people about . . . I'd just like a minute or two to hear what you think.'

Don't take their name until the end of the short interview. Get them talking first: ask for their opinions and leave checking their name, age, occupation and where they're from until the end. Be sure of the style your publication uses before you set out – some will simply want names and ages, others will want occupations and where interviewees live.

Ring-rounds

These are a variation of the vox pop – but done on the phone. Rather than approaching strangers at random you're calling specific people –

like florists, estate agents or the residents of a particular area. To give the quotes authenticity, make sure you preserve the words and speech patterns of the people you interview. A good shorthand note is key.

Press release follow-ups

Some publications print press releases verbatim (please don't) while others use them as the starting point for their own story. The journalist reads the release, then gets on the phone and starts asking questions. At the very least the journalist will angle the story to suit the readers, and will source their own quotes.

If there is a negative story to unearth, some PRs believe they can hide it either by boring journalists to death or by avoiding the issue altogether. Read the press release carefully to spot where the gaps are, and note down the questions you want to ask. PRs are keen to get coverage, so they will usually put you in touch with interviewees.

Press conferences

The rowdy scrums seen in movies such as 'Notting Hill' are long gone. These days press conferences are tightly controlled and staged by PRs. It's always best to arrive early and check the exact format of the press conference. Will speakers be dashing away afterwards? Or will they be available for private questioning and, if so, for how long? Make sure you get any hand-outs on offer. PRs often prefer to give out press releases after the press conference – to make sure journalists don't simply grab the hand-outs and not bother to sit through the event.

Even if detailed press releases are available, always make notes. Speakers often go off-script, and you may get livelier quotes at unscripted moments. Also, there may be points or statistics mentioned that aren't in the hand-out at all.

Try to sit at the front – so you can see everything and don't miss what's going on. When you ask a question, give your name and the publication you are working for. Don't be afraid to ask simple questions. If the speaker mentions a term you're unfamiliar with, and you don't want to show your ignorance, check it with the PR later. Journalists dislike appearing stupid or uninformed in front of their peers, but it's much more important not to appear stupid in print.

Most journalists hate to ask their best questions in front of their rivals at a press conference, allowing everyone to benefit from the answer. They'd far rather talk to the main speaker one-to-one and get a potential exclusive. Not surprisingly, after the conference there'll usually be a queue of journalists waiting to talk to the speaker on their own. Sometimes other journalists cluster round, and the best plan then is to wait until everyone else, or at least your main competitor, has gone. Otherwise, if your deadline allows, ask the speaker or PR for a separate interview.

If you have no alternative but to ask your best question in public, one ploy is to wait until the conference is nearly over and most questioners are flagging. It is possible that by this stage people will have switched off and are reading their notes instead of listening to your dazzling question.

Online awareness

Most of the advice here and in the rest of the book applies equally to interviewing for online magazines and newsletters – but there are differences when using the internet to conduct an interview, and these relate mostly to the equipment set-up, and the length and style of the questions. Guidelines on these, and other valuable pointers – including outlets for freelance interviews – are found on pages 110–19. As James F. Foust (author of *Online Journalism*) writes: 'The internet is simply a new source for journalists – no more, no less; in that way it is no different from the telephone . . .'.

The deeper difference, though, is where there is neither face-to-face nor telephone contact, the interview is conducted purely online, and questions and answers are emailed back and forth. A significant number of journalists intensely dislike this type of online interviewing, and many news editors are concerned (with good reason) that an online 'story' can later turn out to be a mistake, a misreading or a hoax.

An article in the *Guardian* reported that, to mark its 120th anniversary, the Eiffel Tower in Paris was to have a temporary structure added to the top, designed by architects who had won a competition run by the tower's operation company.

Alas, this was not true. There had been no competition. No planned designs had been announced – though a firm of architects had produced a design. The trouble was that the writer was too eager to get the story published. He didn't contact the architects. 'I went on a lot of architectural forums and I fitted the jigsaw together. I thought it was genuine because I saw it in so many other places,' he said. He didn't check with the tower authorities either. It was Easter Sunday. He 'assumed that they wouldn't be around'.

An aside: mercifully, lessons such as this are often learned early, during training. Don, a social worker, agreed to be interviewed about his work with rent boys. One trainee reporter assumed that Don was a rent boy. Not a good start to the interview. Roz, a novelist, agreed to be interviewed about nearly being killed in Thailand. Another trainee assumed from the start that it was her fault. She was not pleased. Both interviewees still remember the experience – indignantly. Beware of assuming.

Back to journalists who dislike online interviews. 'Lazy journalism,' some say. 'Sterile.' 'It's not an interview at all.' 'An interview consists of two parts: discovery and scrutiny.' 'Too much power for the interviewee.' 'It eliminates the candour, spontaneity and natural dialogue.' These people even differentiate, using punctuation: an interview and an 'interview'.

Opposing them are the growing number of pro-email interviewers. 'Increasingly popular,' they say. 'Puts an end to endless phone calls.' 'Better than knee-jerk responses.' 'Offers well-thought-out answers.' 'Better for very busy men.' 'Great for journalists with woeful shorthand.'

One certainty is that email interviews need planning. Badly handled, they're a waste of your time. So, when fixing one up, make sure, gently but firmly, that your follow-up questions are going to be answered, otherwise you might as well ask for a press release. Best make your opening question a soft one, which they can answer with aplomb – it encourages them enormously.

From this point on, do a 'Spamalot' and look on the bright side. Your interviewees believe they're in charge, so they feel more confident from the very start, and confidence often encourages relaxation or, at the best, indiscretion, producing good, lively quotes.

You also have more time to study email interviewees' answers than you'd have on the phone or face-to-face. You don't have to type out loads of notes. If you have global interviewees, email can save you from having to interview them at 2–3 am.

Of course, the quality of the questions you ask is all-important. So think, think, and go on thinking. It's likely your email interviewee will think more carefully, too, and take longer to answer your questions than they would face-to-face. What they tell you will be, or ought to be, free of mistakes, so there will be no misquoting and you'll have no plaintive 'let-me-see-the-copy-first' pleas. Whatever they write, always remember that it's still *you* who decides what to print and what to cut.

3 Preparing for interviews

Face-to-face and telephone

Successful interviewing is based on being ready for anything and everything that might happen – and that requires a great deal of preparation, particularly for face-to-face. The result: confidence based firmly on research, forethought and planning. And it pays off, sometimes spectacularly.

Ginny Dougary, a journalist who writes for the *Times*, interviewed Felix Dennis, a rich publisher. The interview lasted five hours, followed by dinner. Along the way, Dennis told Dougary: 'I've killed a man.'

Dougary is an interviewer with many years of experience. Just a few weeks before her interview with Dennis she had written about the pitfalls of interviewing. 'Most celebrities these days are too fearful of letting their guard down to have a drink with their interviewer,' she wrote. 'If you are lucky enough to get a good scoop out of such an encounter, unsympathetic commentators may assume that the interviewer has plied their subject with alcohol to exploit the poor vulnerable creature. This is irritating but also nonsense. Revealing interviews, in my experience anyway, have come about because the interviewee finds it a relief to vent or unburden themselves.'

She says she chose to interview Dennis 'for no other reason than that he is colourful, flamboyant, rich and powerful, and has been outspoken already about his louche past'.

The amazing Dougary/Dennis story requires more space than is available here. It's too good and too valuable to condense into a few words. The text of the interview and the resulting correspondence in the British press and online are to be found on Google. They are truly rewarding, and should be read by anyone seeking a lesson in interviewing.

Spending as much time as you can spare to research, prepare and plan is essential. Consider how Ruby Wax approached an interview with

Imelda Marcos, former First Lady of the Philippines, who was said to have a thousand pairs of shoes and was known to be a difficult subject. Wax had been granted 15 minutes, not a second more. She prepared shrewdly.

In her book *How Do You Want Me?*, Wax reports: 'Like most movie stars she started out treating her interviewer (me) like dirt for being a mere mortal. Luckily, I knew this was coming so I borrowed £150,000 of Theo Fennel jewels so that she would at least respect my rocks.' That, and finding that Wax's picture was on the front of *Hello!* made all the difference for Imelda. 'Suddenly she realised I too was sprinkled in celebrity dust.' The result: Wax got the interview. Those 15 minutes turned into three days.

Planning

Planning is a vital part of preparation, whether for face-to-face, telephone or online interviews. Face-to-face is the most complex and demanding, and the basis on which telephone interviews are planned, so it's covered here first.

Bill Browne, now publisher of the *Salisbury Journal*, recounts:

> As a really wet-behind-the-ears junior I was told at 10 minutes notice to go to a bookshop and interview a famous author. So famous that I didn't know what she'd done [sailed round the world single-handed].
>
> I walked in with a general question like 'Can you tell me about your interest in sailing?' and she said: 'You obviously haven't done any research.' There was a pause and she added: 'Now he's trying to think of something sensible to ask me.'
>
> The fault was mine. I could have stopped by the library on the way to the bookshop, taken five minutes to look at the clips. It was my first celebrity interview. The best lesson I could ever have had.

Persist

Once you know who you are interviewing, you need to persuade them to talk to you. It helps to have a good reputation and to work for a highly rated publication. Even then, persistence is important.

Newly arrived from Australia, Phillip Knightley was freelancing for the *Sunday Times*. On one occasion, given a good lead, he failed to get the interview and received the following advice from a colleague, which, he says, had a resounding effect on his career: 'Most people are modest or like to give that impression. So when you want to put them in the limelight they'll say no. But they don't mean it. They're waiting for you to ask again, so that they can surrender gracefully and modestly. In journalism, no "no" is ever final.'

What can you do if you're unknown and work on an unappealing title? First, put on your target's shoes and try to work out what will persuade them to drop their defences. It could be publicity, exposure, a raised profile, perhaps the opportunity to put their side of a story or to correct inaccuracies. You have to persuade them of your worth and your substance, too.

If you're approaching a person, company or organisation with an agent or PR, you can phone, email or write, putting your request in a positive light. It took me a day to write the letter that got me onto a nuclear submarine. I dredged my background to offer proof that would allay the fears in the naval mind about freelance journalists. Writing direct to the person works well. You can always ask an intermediary to vouch for you, or mention their name when you write (check with your referee first, of course).

Writing long-term pays off, too. Phillip Knightley corresponded with the spy Kim Philby for more than 20 years before getting an interview with him in Moscow, just before Philby died. Politicians, gifted with a keen sense of priority, may put on hold interviews with publications they see as tangential to their immediate interests. It took two years of persistent reminders by Nick Pigott, then editor of *Railway* magazine, before the then secretary of state for the environment, transport and the regions made good his promise of an exclusive interview.

Enterprise pays off

An aviation chief executive was involved in a tremendous brouhaha and found himself besieged by phone calls from the press. He ducked into the trenches and let his secretary take the calls, refusing every request for an interview. Over the course of the next few days, his secretary came to know several members of the press. Turning down a journalist's *n*th request for an interview, she told her that the executive had just left the factory to catch a train to London for a meeting.

The journalist knew where the factory was, consulted the timetable, and met the train. Waiting at the barrier, she recognised him from his photograph. 'Mr . . .,' she greeted him, 'I'm from the *Daily*. . . . Could you spare me some time?' Deeply impressed, he agreed. Of such are scoops made.

As a last resort, when a previously much-written-about person has gone to ground, you could try this. A powerful businessman about to retire refused all requests for an interview from *Financial Times* journalist Ken Gooding. Gooding went through the file and picked out all the peculiarities ever written about the man but which had never been denied: that he always walked to work but made his chauffeur follow him in the car; that he wore a pink rose in his buttonhole on Mondays, a yellow one on Tuesdays . . .

> I picked out all the stupid bits and made him look the most bizarre person in the world, then sent the copy round. He was on the phone within five minutes . . . Of course, a more sophisticated person might have got his lawyer on the phone.

A time and a place

Most appointments are made and confirmed on the phone. As you can't see what your interviewee or their secretary/PA is doing, it's wise to be pernickety.

First, you need to identify yourself and your publication, give them an idea of what you want to talk to them about and a rough idea of how long it might take. It's important to phrase your request so that they sense how they'll benefit. A proper sense of urgency and pride in your publication helps.

Be especially careful to check the date and day of the week of your appointment. You might not be looking at the wrong month in your diary, but your interviewee might. So follow up with: 'That's Wednesday, 14 October, at 3.30pm – right?'

Interviews over lunch go well, especially when lubricated with alcohol, but you need either a quiet restaurant and a good recorder with a directional mike or the ability to take notes while you eat one-handed, which limits what you order.

Few people now have the time to eat first and be interviewed afterwards, and anyway, if you appear at all interested in them, they're bound to say something quotable while eating, so you'd have to get out your notebook or recorder anyhow. Beware of crowded pubs, cafés, theatre lobbies, anywhere with music.

You may ask them for 40 minutes and the interviewee says: 'Sorry – I can spare you just 15.' At this point you have to decide whether to risk offending them by asking for extra time, thus getting off on the wrong foot. Alternatively, accept what they offer and make sure the interview is really interesting. Then, unless you're dealing with an important executive, or someone on a fixed timetable or with a subsequent appointment, you're likely to be given your extra time.

A Radio Five Live presenter told one freelance he could spare a quarter of an hour. Forty-five minutes later they were still talking and, at the end of the interview, the freelance mentioned he'd been generous with his time. 'Just wanted to be able to get rid of you if necessary,' the presenter said.

Many people are more benevolent, chatty and relaxed after lunch so, if the interviewee or the subject is likely to be tricky, try for the afternoon. Your place or mine? No contest: theirs. They'll feel more at home and you can see the house, desk, factory, workshop, studio – and how they relate to the people around them.

If necessary, establish how to get there. Be very careful when taking down instructions. Never, ever, accept those that start 'Take the second on the right after you go under the bridge', for the obvious reasons that (a) there may be more than one bridge, and (b) you or your interviewee may not know from which direction you will approach the bridge. Bitter experience speaking.

Ask for, and get, road names. This helps cut out the mistakes which occur when you're told 'take the third on the left', whereas it's really the fourth but your interviewee can't count, has never noticed one of the roads, or doesn't rate it.

Finally, when scheduling appointments, be sure to make contingency plans: exchange mobile phone numbers, so you can reach one another if either of you has to cancel.

What to take with you

Before you leave for the interview, check you've got what you need. Put everything in a neat file, briefcase or bag. Whatever you do, don't arrive with shopping or your belongings in a load of carrier bags – you'll simply look unprofessional.

Don't forget the following:

- Notebook (plus a spare if the current one is nearly full). Some journalists prefer the traditional spiral-bound reporter's notebooks, but others choose larger ones, especially for longer interviews.
- Pens/pencils.
- Recorder, fully charged and ready to go or with sufficient spare batteries.
- Headphones (to check the player is working properly and, if your deadline is tight, to enable you to start transcribing the interview on the way back to the office).
- Mobile phone.
- Business cards.
- Change for parking meters, etc.
- Address, telephone number and email details of the interviewee.
- Map/directions on how to get there.
- Copy of the publication you're writing for.
- Background research (just in case you're early and have time to glance at it again).

It's important to dress suitably and in a way that suits both the occasion and the publication you represent. Politicians and businesspeople usually wear suits, so it's a great mistake to arrive for an interview with them dressed in T-shirt and jeans. Likewise, if you're interviewing an up-and-coming rock band, a business suit and tie might be over the top.

Emma Lee-Potter, a freelance journalist, recalls when one of her colleagues arrived for work in a polo-neck and jeans at the small weekly paper where they were both trainee reporters. He was immediately sent home to change by the irate editor, who told him: 'How could I send you to interview the Archbishop of Canterbury looking like that?'

Freelance writer and editor Melanie Whitehouse says it's vital to dress appropriately. 'When I interviewed the writer Barbara Cartland I made sure I wore a pink blouse, long pleated skirt, boots, a romantic-looking coat and Dr Zhivago-style fake fur hat. She knew exactly what I was doing but she appreciated it and it made the interview that much easier and more productive. In short, play the game and you'll be the winner.'

Planning the interview

Once the subject of the news story, or the approach and angle of the feature, has been agreed, it's time to gather your facts. For news, begin with the Who? What? Where? When, Why? How? approach. For feature interviews, once the preliminary brief has been agreed, start your research.

If your topic is general, for example, the food hygiene regulations governing street markets, or how to edit a parish magazine, you might need to do some research to find experts who are articulate and willing to talk.

If your subject is an individual, for example, a politician or the star of a new TV soap, you need to find out more about them by talking to their fans or detractors, agents or directors, partners and friends.

Look on the internet, in the cuttings, in other publications, in books and encyclopaedias. Talk to colleagues, contacts, competitors, PRs, friends, enemies, relatives, neighbours. Check with the company, the organisation, the society – demand information anywhere and everywhere. Note what you find and where you found it, and always remember that information is only as good as the source; the internet is *not* always reliable.

Suppose your topic is 'weather forecasting', a huge subject with a gigantic cast of characters. You could spend weeks, perhaps months, reading around the subject, but you haven't the time. So start with a quick look at an official meteorological website or an encyclopaedia reference. Find the names of some experts and phone them. Somewhere there is someone who is, in effect, a search engine on the subject, someone who can point you towards the most knowledgeable amateur, the most eccentric rainfall measurer in Iceland, the academic researching the most esoteric aspect of storms, TV weather forecasters in Papua New Guinea, etc.

Read everything you can, then pause. Turn yourself into your editor/ features editor and your readers. What would they want to know? Pause again. Ask yourself what hasn't been covered? What doesn't hang together? Where are the gaps, the cracks? What questions hasn't this person answered yet?

This is where the fresh, the unexpected questions are formulated: questions that yield new, revealing, startling quotes or facts. It's by knowing the old angle that you get the new angle.

Inadequate research means you can miss the story. A business-to-business (B2B) magazine commissioned freelance Janet Barber to interview the head of a local organisation. Back at the office after the interview, she mentioned she'd just talked to him, and a colleague said: 'Oh yes, he's the one who had a brick thrown through his window, isn't he?' Her man had been linked with a terrorist group, something she knew nothing about. 'So I had to phone him back, check, and as a result I got a much better interview. Now I check with as many sources as I can, particularly colleagues,' says Barber.

Sometimes her subjects turned out to be elusive. One of the most evasive was an official at a political party's central office.

> It was an uphill task. The unhelpfulness of their press office was absolutely unbelievable. They would not give me any information at all. I tried colleagues. I had to ask around, does anybody know him? Do they know what he looks like?
>
> I sat down and really worked the phone. I got lift-off when I finally found someone who knew him who was willing to talk on the record. I had to be able to quote people by name, at least three or four of them, though I used info from the rest as background.
>
> In the end it made a cover story but we couldn't get a photo specially taken; we had to blow up a conference photo of him with someone else. Later one of my colleagues took him out to lunch and he said: 'She managed very well, considering we wouldn't give her any help at all.'

What to ask

Research gives you the angle and points up the areas to cover. By this time you will have established what you want to know: what combination of information (facts, names, details), opinion (quotes), background (context) and anecdotes.

You must then work out what areas you want to cover, what questions you want to ask. (Questions – formulating them, revising them, asking them – are discussed at length in Chapter 4.) Interview planning includes deciding what topics to cover and how many questions to prepare: as many as you think seems right, with several left over for emergencies, is safest. 'A question for every line in my notebook,' one journalist told me. If in doubt, err on the long side.

Obviously, you must obtain your publication's 'must-know' facts: name, job title, exact name of employing company, annual turnover (for a journal such as *Business Week*, for example); name, age, occupation and where they live (for a local paper); name, location, hectarage of farm, number/breed of cows in the herd (*Dairy Farmer*); price per square metre of carpet, fibre, manufacturer (*Floors and Floor Covering*). Make sure you get the spelling right. Exchanging business cards and reading annual reports often yields much basic info. Then you need to work out how best to find the answers to whatever else you need to cover.

Write your topics/questions down on a separate sheet of paper. If you're using a notebook and doing a business interview, and you need to know such things as last year's turnover and the percentage increase/fall over the previous year (exports by value; exports by volume, etc.), it's a good idea to number these questions and then put that number against the answer during the interview. This avoids finding lots of statistics when you come back to your notebook but not having a clear memory of which question they refer to.

Though it's vital to go into the interview with your topics and questions prepared, it's equally vital to be ready to rephrase them to suit your interviewee once you start. And never forget that, all the time you're talking, they're probably trying to work out how the interview will look in print. If they can't see any advantage to themselves, they may become cagey – the last thing you want.

When to arrive

Arrive on time or slightly early, even though you may be kept waiting. To be late is unforgivable so, when you set out, allow for possible delays.

Once, reporting for a Third World charity quarterly, I found the lift out of order at the interviewee's building and had to climb three flights of stairs. I've still not forgotten the embarrassment of reaching fund-raiser James Tysoe's office as the hour struck, only to be shown straight in having collected neither my thoughts nor my breath. Flustered is not a good way to start an interview.

Obviously you can be more relaxed if you're driving across country to interview someone at their home. But tycoons, PRs running celebrity junkets, managers and businesspeople all work to tight schedules, and it's vital to be there for your slot or you may lose it.

If you are late, don't assume all is lost. The best way to avert wrath is to call en route to let them know you've been held up – which is why you have your mobile phone and their contact number with you.

And now . . .

You've done all your research and thought of a fresh and lively angle; you've prepared your topics and questions carefully and are ready to rephrase them to suit your interviewee; you've packed your recorder, notebooks, pens, pencils, etc.; you know where you're going; you're dressed like the sort of person your interviewee will talk to.

You've set off in good time, making allowances for traffic and potential hold-ups. All your efforts must now concentrate on the interviewee. They are the star of the interview, and anything – truly anything – that suggests to them that you're not making them central to the encounter could damage, maybe even ruin, the interview. Leave your ego at the door.

The interview starts

First impressions count. TV dramatist Andrea Newman was once interviewed by seven journalists in one day. She says that, by interviewer number five, she knew in the first few seconds if the interview would work. One writer walked into the hall, sniffed dismissively, and commented 'Ummmm'. It was a short interview.

Nerves and lack of practice handicap the beginner. To make a good first impression, it's necessary to come through the door in a pleasant but businesslike way. If you're seeing someone at their place of work you may be asked to wait. Resist all impulses to unpack your bag and recheck you've got everything you need. Sod's law will spring into operation and, just as everything is scattered about, the interviewee will turn up in person.

Settle down to wait, confident that you prepared well, and look forward to meeting your interviewee. It's wise to read any company literature offered and look around the reception area for clues about your interviewee or the company. Of course listen to any conversations going on around you.

You may be ushered in by a secretary or an assistant, or you may just be pointed towards a door. Though the following advice may sound corny – too much like the PE teacher's warm-up routine – try it if you're at all nervous. As you approach the door, take a deep breath, stand tall and pull your shoulders back.

If you're expected, there's no need to knock and wait. Walk in, right up to the interviewee. If you lurk close to the door you give off the wrong signal. You're there as a journalist, not a supplicant.

However anxious you are, walking in looking worried is counterproductive. Be pleased to see your interviewee. That means looking at them and smiling – and if you don't realise this naturally, perhaps you should rethink your career choice.

Shaking hands

The first anxiety for some beginners when they come face-to-face with their interviewee is whether or not to shake hands. If your interviewee advances, hand outstretched, take it without hesitation. Should the interviewee make no gesture either way, then it's up to you. Shaking hands seems sensible, since it can be revealing, but if your hand is clammy from nerves, brush or rub it dry on your trousers or skirt as you step forward.

Most handshakes are unremarkable, but occasionally, when you interview a businessman for example, you may experience the truly surprising dominant 'palm down' power shake. Your hand is grasped firmly, somehow turned palm up, then given a sharp shake. Weird.

There's also the 'politician's' handshake, in which their two hands cover your one. This is usually diagnosed as a wish to project honesty. An add-on is the left hand grasping your elbow or upper arm at the same time, interpreted as a desire to convey honesty plus concern and warmth. Of course, some people have less assertive handshakes from necessity or expedience: they may have arthritis, for example, or they use their hands to make a living – such as pianists, puppeteers, embroiderers and surgeons.

Eye contact

How and how much you look at your interviewee matters vitally – look, please, but don't stare. Whether they realise it or not, it affects how much they will tell you. Look at them and they know they have your interest. Continue looking and they know they have your full attention, which is flattering. Smile, too: a simple, unforced, pleased-to-meet-you smile. Smiling makes people who smile feel better, so it works in your favour, and it will also reassure your interviewee. An anxious scowl gets everything off to a poor start.

What to call them? If in doubt it's safer to be formal – 'Mr', 'Mrs' or 'Ms'. Some interviewees loathe informality, and using their first name without invitation prejudices them against you immediately. If they're happy with informality they'll soon let you know. Only one more ritual to observe. If you haven't already done so, introduce yourself, giving your name and publication.

Where to sit

Don't be in a hurry at this stage. I'd recommend that you don't sit down until you're asked to (it gives them a warm feeling that they're in charge). Take your time before you begin. One good way to start is to thank the interviewee for seeing you. Some journalists won't do this on principle, reasoning that the interviewees aren't doing them a favour but hoping to gain from the transaction. However, from the journalist's viewpoint it's a wise move. Like smiling, it suggests interest and pleasure. It reassures the nervous and encourages the uncertain.

If this is your first interview, sit where indicated. Later, with growing experience and confidence, you can be more choosy – because where you sit matters. Accepted wisdom is that sitting directly opposite your interviewee is a mistake. It's confrontational, the chess or 'war' position.

Sitting too far away is a mistake, too, as is sitting side by side on the sofa. This is gruesomely matey, and pure agony if you use shorthand or combined recorder and notes, since the interviewee has only to throw in a few statistics, names or trade marks to see exactly what you're taking down and how far behind you are.

There's general agreement that sitting at about right-angles (90°) works best, being neither confrontational nor cosy. As you grow more confident, with business interviews especially, avoid any chair that's lower than your interviewee's, since that puts you in a subordinate position. No need for the contrary advice – it won't happen.

If, when you're a more experienced interviewer, you are directed to a seat on the executive sofa and would prefer to avoid it, say something along the lines of 'If it's OK with you, I'd prefer to sit here' (indicating where). Only the truly cussed interviewee would demur.

At ease

Your next task is to build rapport, which is easier than it sounds. You started when you greeted them warmly and thanked them for agreeing to see you. Now you need to say something that makes them look kindly on you.

The easiest way to build rapport is to establish common ground: to mention something, experience, attitude or belief you both share and agree on. There's no one sure method. It varies from interviewee to interviewee. If you know from their CV that they went to the same university as you did, say so. You went to Bristol/Oxford/Manchester/York/London University? You're more than OK. You come with a positive stamp of approval.

Other possibilities: if their company has just pulled off a major acquisition against long odds, offer congratulations. Praise, aka flattery, never goes amiss. If the view from their window is stunning, you could say so. If they have a Burmese cat, and your auntie has one too, tell them. Establish a community of likes. Make yourself agreeable in a way that shows you see them as an interesting person, not just a potential source to be squeezed dry of facts in as short a time as possible.

As you become more experienced, there's another way to establish rapport: mirror their body language. If they sit back relaxed, you sit back relaxed. If they lean forward, you lean forward. If they cross their legs, you cross your legs. Be warned: it needs to be subtly done. Don't try this until you're at ease with the interview process or you'll do it clumsily and it will be so obvious that it won't work – like the synchronised swimming team's first practice session, in fact.

Matching the interviewee's rate of speaking also works, both to establish rapport and to make the interview flow smoothly throughout, and this is easier to achieve.

When to begin

It's said that most people make up their minds in the first four minutes after being introduced, so within that time a mixture of charm and getting down to business is recommended – unless the discussion about the university, takeover, view or cat is going so well it would be crass to interrupt. The interview proper has yet to begin, though that doesn't mean everything said earlier doesn't count. Your interviewee may be quite nervous and need time to settle down, or may prattle away confidently from the first. Either way, sooner or later – and you must be the judge of when – there will come a time when you begin. It's your interview.

You are – and must be – in charge. However subtly it's done, you call the shots. If you don't, you may end up writing at their dictation or being borne off on a flood of useless reminiscence, unable to stop the flow. For some fact-heavy, structured interviews the control needs to be tight, but many interviewers find they get the best quotes by using a firm hand in a very velvety glove.

You walked through the door knowing what you wanted to get out of the interview. It is up to you whether you walk out with mission accomplished or not.

Down to business

Time to get out your notebook or recorder. Unless you're dealing with someone who's very nervous, there's no need to apologise or ask permission. If you have any doubts, say something like 'You've no objection to a recorder, I trust.' Make it a statement rather than a question. Now's the time, too, to give them your business card if you have one.

Before launching into the interview, it's important that you should remind them of what you want to talk about. This is true whether they are a top-flight professional doing six interviews a day or someone being interviewed for the first time. Repeating the interview subject and your angle focuses their minds. It's in your interest that they know. If they don't, they may set off in what for you is a hopeless direction, wasting everyone's time.

Rather than a brusque 'OK, tell me about your snail farm', a softer and wiser approach would be to explain some of the thinking behind the interview. For example, '*Farmers Gazette* readers are very interested in diversification, and your snail farm is one of the most unusual ideas we've heard about. I'm hoping you can give me a picture of where you got the idea, about your start-up and running costs, the pleasures and pitfalls of snail farming and whether you'd recommend it to other farmers. That sort of thing.'

The idea is to avoid an abrupt jump-start, to give them a little time to collect their thoughts and get ready to answer. Beginners are advised to start gently. If you ask something your interviewee can't answer, they may feel cross with themselves and, most likely, furious with you too. Either way it's a bad idea.

For several reasons, beginners are advised to start by asking about their 'must-know' facts. First, because these are safe and easy to confirm. Second, because they reassure the interviewee, dealing as they do with accurate checking. Third, because by the end of the interview the first-time interviewer may be so exhausted or elated that they forget to ask. It happens. And so does the embarrassing follow-up phone call. 'Hello, it's . . . again. Sorry to bother you, but I forgot to check so-and-so.'

Again, don't start abruptly. Plunging in with: 'What's your name and how do you spell it?' isn't recommended. Much better, as suggested in Chapter 4, is to say: 'I'd like to start by checking how you spell your name.' You're aiming for an interview that runs smoothly, where your interviewee feels at ease.

Here's how not to start from Maggie Craig, novelist and writer of non-fiction

> 'So,' asked the young journalist as she sat down at my kitchen table, 'what would you say to those people who say that the sort of books you write are written for housewives who are not very well educated?'
>
> As an opening gambit it fair took the biscuit. Hell, it took the best all-butter shortbread I had bought in for her visit. 'Have you,' I asked mildly, 'read any of my books?'
>
> Go on. Take a wild guess as to what her answer was . . .
>
> (*Author* magazine)

Make it interesting – for them

Empathy, rather than sympathy, is a prime requirement for interviewers. Until you've been interviewed by a succession of journalists relentlessly pumping you for information or quotes, you can have no idea how boring being asked the same questions can be – especially if the answers elicit no response except the next speedy, predictable question.

Shirley Conran, an accomplished self-publicist, went round the world promoting her books and said about her first bestseller, *Lace*, that interviewers only ever asked four questions – and one of them was 'always about the goldfish'.

So be sure to make the interview a pleasure for your subject. This means engaging their interest from the start. Early on, ask something that shows you're not just another hack, routinely asking predictable questions.

Doctors have 'heart-sink' patients who visit the surgery every day – the doctor's heart sinks at the sight of them. Avoid being a 'heart-sink' questioner, signalling from the beginning that the interview is to cover well-trampled ground. The interviewee subconsciously switches off, gives well-rehearsed answers and functions on automatic pilot – exactly what shouldn't happen.

4 Interviewing techniques

Here's that rare thing, a chapter on interviewing techniques that doesn't start with questions. That's because the main purpose of a print interview is to get the interviewee talking freely, and the best way to do that is to listen.

As American writer John Brady put it: 'No talking journalist ever held a good interview.' The description of an interview as 'a conversation with a purpose' is misleading, unless what's in mind is a cleverly guided, very one-sided conversation.

Interviewers need to master the non-questioning skills of eliciting information and quotes. These are:

- Listen and encourage.
- Use silence.
- Make statements requiring confirmation/denial.
- Summarise and move on.

There is good reason for this apparently perverse order, starting as it does with the 'mute' techniques. Listening and encouraging people to talk are not the simple skills they seem and should be learned and practised early. Worse, journalists raised on TV and radio interviews and who have received little or no specialist training may not even believe such techniques exist, and instead adopt the rapid-fire, ping-pong Q&A style that is quite wrong for print journalists.

The first injunction is to be flexible. The aim is to get your interviewee to drop their defences. This means you have to adapt your approach to suit them – calm the excitable, reassure the uncertain and steer the confident and knowledgeable.

Good interviewers are long-time people-watchers and eavesdroppers. They look, they listen. They ask themselves: what does that gesture mean; why did they look down then; why such a dramatic response to such a casual question; are those two squaring up for a row; why doesn't she interrupt him; who's the dominant person in that group; what do those three have in common?

If they can, they stick around to check if their answers are right. Fans of the movies score well here, as do actors-turned-writers, for obvious reasons. They listen, they watch, they analyse.

If there's one motto that interviewers should adopt it's this: *You get more flies with honey than vinegar*. Being nice works better than being nasty almost every time – and certainly to begin with.

Listen and encourage

One of life's ironies is that, of the four great communicating skills – listening, speaking, reading and writing – the one that is learnt first, listening, is taught least, while writing, which is learnt last, is taught most. Listening requires immense concentration and is exhausting. Anyone aiming for a face-to-face interview longer than an hour is advised to take a break, for their own sake as well as the interviewee's.

Listening also requires empathy, discipline, understanding and patience. If you're tense, indifferent, hostile, impatient or distracted, you won't listen well. The best listeners, rather like the best reportage photographers, are self-effacing. They concentrate on their interviewees so much that they almost become invisible. One sign of good interviewers is that, strangely, they're forgotten.

Listening is not the same as hearing. Good listening is hearing and understanding. In face-to-face interviews it means you are interested in what's being said and show it clearly – so you should look at your interviewee. Although it's possible to listen to someone with your back to them, they will hate it, and, being uncertain of your attention, will dry up. In phone interviews, the equivalent of showing that you're listening is to use lots of positive 'ums' and 'ahs' and 'yeses'.

Interviewees won't maintain steady eye contact with you, but they need to know when they check back – as they do at irregular intervals – that you're concentrating on them. Lynda Lee-Potter said that, if you take your eyes off them for even a split second, you can hear their voices start to falter. Celebrities often have a greater need than most to be looked at because they're used to it and it reassures them. Some are said to storm out the minute they find the interviewer is not looking at them.

Once you have got people talking, you need to encourage them to continue – for example, by using reassuring body language: mirroring their posture in the first place, using nods, head tilts, leaning forward and smiling. Mirroring their posture is subliminal reassurance. Nods are much more noticeable, a sign that you hear and understand. Nods can come singly, in pairs or threes. More than that can be seen as overdoing it and can be interpreted as a signal that you wish to interrupt or are bored.

If you're not a natural nodder, watch others, practise and, before you add nodding to your interview techniques, check how comfortable you look in a mirror. Too many forced nods look ridiculous and inhibit rather than encourage your interviewee.

The vocalised version, the 'uh-huh' – often accompanied by an almost invisible nod – is another great encourager. It's very useful in face-to-face interviews and essential on the telephone. Used liberally, it helps answers to flow freely. The American version of the British 'uh-huh' is 'uh-ah', which rises on the last syllable and is much more upbeat than the grunt. Used repeatedly, as verbal encouragers tend to be during interviews, 'uh-huh' is definitely preferable to repeatedly spoken words or phrases such as 'right', 'yes', 'that so?', 'I see'. Singly, they work. Too many and they become a huge irritant.

Head tilts – putting your head on one side – come naturally to some. They're a way of saying 'Please carry on'. If you watch people listening to young children you'll see head tilts most of the time. The listener silently encourages the child to continue, sending out an 'I'm hearing you' message.

Leaning forward is another way of showing how engaged you are. Like mirroring the interviewee's body language, it broadcasts a subconscious approval message. Smiling adds further reassurance. The opposite of all of these – an impassive, non-responsive, stony-faced, bored-looking interviewer – sends out all the wrong messages, messages that are certain to be received at some level.

Use silence

It's impossible to overemphasise the importance of silence. Not in the first few minutes of the interview, of course, when you're establishing your credentials, or if you have a nervous, over-talkative interviewee; but once they have taken your measure, relaxed and started to talk easily, then you must talk very little.

It's difficult to be silent – agin nature for some journalists – but it's one of the most valuable techniques. So get into the habit of not jumping in with another question or comment as soon as the interviewee has finished speaking. Instead, count at least four seconds silently to yourself. You'll be amazed how often the interviewee carries on speaking, amplifying their last comment. Most of us discover this for the first time when we are stumped for what to ask next, and are astonished to find our interviewee doesn't seem to have realised but carries on speaking as though nothing has happened.

For those who are unsure how long four seconds lasts, it's about the time you can say to yourself 'One Mississippi, two Mississippi, three Mississippi, four Mississippi'. However ill at ease you feel, persevere. I opted for a four-second pause some years ago, mostly on a gut feel. It seemed the right amount of time to allow before continuing. It was gratifying to learn while researching this book that three seconds is the time it takes most people to frame replies. Don't overdo it and use really long silences, though. They're counter-productive, leading to short answers from puzzled, anxious or mystified interviewees.

If you need extra persuasion to keep silent, bear in mind that the more you interrupt, the less you listen and the less they will talk. What to listen for? Everything, really. First, the exact words the interviewee uses, then their eagerness or reluctance to answer particular questions, the tone or strength of voice, any pauses, omissions, where they become animated, where they sound reluctant . . .

Listening to precisely what is said is particularly important if the interviewee is well practised in dealing with journalists. In these days of sophisticated news management, many interviewees are trained in how to respond to unwelcome questions. They know that the truth and nothing but the truth is easy but that the whole truth is the killer. So given a choice between lying, fudging, evading or telling the truth, the adept will opt for a limited amount of the truth, because it's easy to remember and a great protection. That's why listening to *exactly* what they say is essential.

A famous politician in his early days, eager to be adopted as a candidate for a safe constituency, is said to have included in his application details a list of all the articles he had written for the *Guardian*, neatly omitting the fact that none had actually been published.

Examples:

> 'The chairman studied archaeology at Cambridge.'

Don't presume he or she got a degree in archaeology: they may have studied it but failed finals.

And my particular favourite:

> 'Our budget? Well, it's under a million.'

from a producer replying to queries about his first film, which had a budget of £11,000.

A story is told about General de Gaulle, one-time president of France. After Britain had devalued the pound, there was heavy pressure on France to follow suit. Under questioning, de Gaulle said he would devalue the franc by somewhere between 0 per cent and 5 per cent. This answer bought him – and the franc – time, and pressure for action eased. He then did exactly what he had said he would do: he devalued the franc by 0 per cent.

One clue to the limited-truth reply is that the interviewee often rephrases the question in answering. Suppose the question is:

> 'When was the first time you heard he'd quit as manager?'

and the answer comes:

> 'I was gobsmacked to hear him talking about it on the radio on Monday morning.'

The reply may be true, but it doesn't answer the question. Politicians are great exponents of rephrasing when they answer, as it enables them to respond to a difficult question smoothly.

Listening attentively is an obvious compliment to the interviewee. It also allows you to collect the information you're after and ask intelligent supplementary questions. The converse – not paying attention, not asking obvious follow-up questions but rather ones that are random and inconsequential – offends interviewees and is one of the prime reasons for interviews being cut short.

Particularly during long interviews, you should listen for changes in the strength of voice or speed of talking. Dropping or lowering tone and slowing down usually mean you've reached something significant about which the interviewee has reservations of some sort, usually emotional. Raising or increasing the volume generally signifies positive, tell-the-world content.

Make statements requiring confirmation, denial or amplification

Questioning sits on a continuum that ranges from casual checking at one end to interrogation at the other. Considering the power of the press, it's easy to understand why many people are apprehensive about being interviewed.

One way to put them at their ease is not to ask questions but to seek confirmation or amplification. You can do this through statements.

> 'I'd just like to check how you spell your name.'

This is a much better opener than the brusque:

> 'How do you spell your name?'

Similarly:

> 'I see from the cuttings that you have a house in the south-west of France.'

Or:

> 'Friends tell me you have a house in the Charente, in the south-west.'

This approach works surprisingly well when dealing with sports people. At the end of the game or competition, remind them of an important moment – 'that second goal was astonishing' – then wait. You'll get a stream of valuable comments and analysis. Sports people can be more articulate than it sometimes appears. The key is to remind, not ask. Maybe not being asked a question could be exactly the way to get them talking.

The same approach works when wanting amplification from reluctant boasters:

> 'You must have worked very hard to complete the refurbishment ahead of schedule and under budget.'
>
> 'Your customers say your sausages are the finest in Bawtry.'
>
> 'I called your colleague Helen who tells me I must ask about your trip to the South Pole.'
>
> 'I understand it was your idea to develop the annual office outing.'

Having information confirmed usually reassures interviewees that you're getting your facts right, but if you are trying to get them to confirm something not to their advantage, then a question is often wiser. It is easier for them to avoid responding to a statement such as:

> 'I understand there have been a lot of redundancies announced recently.'

than it would be to answer the question:

> 'How many redundancies will there be?'

The guideline here is not to ask questions like this until well into the interview, when the interviewee is talking freely and senses that any avoidance or hesitation would send out a glaring signal of reluctance.

It's also possible to discover information by making statements that require denial. This is much more problematic, because you don't know what negative buttons you are pressing.

> 'There's no smoke without fire, so I take it the rumour that your latest model has hit safety problems is true.'
>
> 'I understand you were once convicted of being drunk and incapable.'

Negative statements can often provoke a lively, vigorous denial, but be sure of your interviewee before you try this too often.

Summarise and move on

One last and valuable type of statement is the summary. Use this when your interviewee is over-talkative or time is running short. Summarise what they have said, restate it, and then you can move on.

> 'So what you're saying is . . . Now I'd like to turn to . . .'
>
> 'Let's see if I've got this right . . . Perhaps we can now talk about . . .'
>
> 'We've covered . . . so next . . .'

Questions

Questions should be framed to achieve their purpose. Maybe this is to reassure the interviewee that you'll spell the name of their company correctly. Maybe it's to signal to them that you know more about their past than they suspect. Maybe it's to encourage them to talk about their favourite subject. Maybe it's to make sure they remember you.

The aim of the questions is vital; so is the way that you frame them and put them. Consider this approach by a journalist who'd just joined the Liverpool *Daily Post* and was sent to cover a fatal industrial accident.

> I put down my pad as aggressively as I could and said: 'Right, let's get the details' – and of course they wouldn't give anything away. Then the chief reporter arrived . . . looking like Columbo with his old mac on. His approach to the manager was: 'I suppose you won't be saying anything about this? Quite, I quite understand.'
>
> But then he had this wonderful way of asking questions without appearing to. Within two minutes he had already framed the first four or five paragraphs. 'I suppose he wouldn't have been here long . . .? Oh, it was his first day.'
>
> I was just standing there gobsmacked . . . You learn a lot about not being demanding and aggressive, not looking as if you knew the answers.

The journalist was John Sergeant, who went on to become ITN's political editor, and who remembered this important lesson years later when interviewed by the *Press Gazette*.

Categories and categorising

You can categorise questions in a number of ways – by purpose, by content, by way of asking – but first let's examine the three recognised main categories: closed, open, and leading. All are valuable when used at the right time in the right way.

Closed

These are commonly defined as questions that can be answered 'yes' or 'no', but a more sensible definition is that they are questions about fact or opinion that can be answered briefly. Closed questions are ideal for establishing essentials – names, job titles, locations – once the interview is under way.

> 'Did you see the accident?'
> 'No.'
>
> 'What's the group's full title?'
> 'The United Bellringers of Scourie.'
>
> 'How many boats can moor at the Marina?'
> '120.'
>
> 'What's her middle name?'
> 'Arabella.'
>
> 'Where was the last AGM held?'
> 'Birmingham.'

Closed questions can be useful if you're very near your deadline, because they speed up replies, but using too many can damp down the interviewee's interest. They move into an answering, not talking, mode. The more closed questions are asked, the shorter the answers to any subsequent open questions will be.

The only people who seem to welcome closed questions are the inarticulate, the nervous and those with nothing to hide. Too many short answers do not a good interview make.

Open

Open questions require more than a few words for a satisfactory answer:

> 'How did the man saw through the bars using just dental floss?'
>
> 'What made you decide to become a Salvation Army officer?'

'Why do you think the pony survived being struck by lightning?'

'Exactly what is the difference between Spanish and Moroccan green olives?'

Among variations of the open question is the *echo*, to be used when you sense that the interviewee might like to say more, but that direct probing might not draw it out. Use this sparingly, and practise first.

They say: 'I went absolutely ballistic.'
You pause – then repeat: 'You went absolutely ballistic?'
You pause again – and ideally they add more.

'I fell in love with him there and then.'
You pause – then repeat: 'You fell in love with him there and then?'
You pause – and ideally they add more.

Amplification

Amplification questions are a sub-category of open questions, used to elicit extra details. The task here is to get the interviewee to supply those all-important vivid or visual examples – the 'for instance' hooks of communication.

'Then I started work for . . ., a Third World charity.'
'What exactly did the job involve?'
'Visiting community development schemes in Zambia and Brazil, talking to the families involved and reporting back to the supporters. I've slept in mud huts in Zambia, helped dispense condoms at an AIDS clinic, and been inside two Brazilian brothels.'

'As a result, the two of them had a dreadful row.'
'Could you tell me more – for instance, were they shouting?'
'Shouting? They were screaming at each other. Richard called Andrew an upper-class prat and Andrew said Richard couldn't find his arse in the dark. Andrew walked out and hasn't been seen since. Richard's confiscated Andrew's mobile and instructed security not to let him into the building.'

'The company's had several bright marketing ideas.'
'Could you describe the three most successful to me?'

Clarification

Clarification questions are another sub-category. The more you interview, the more you realise how important it is to check you've understood what you've been told.

> 'The outcome was so unfair I decided to leave there and then.'
> 'Is that when you went to work on the dictionary?'
> 'No, no, you misunderstand. I left work early that day. I didn't quit the job until later. I was headhunted by Mutel-Morange Ltd.'
> 'That was the same year?'
> 'No – it took a year before I moved.'

The approach here should be along the lines of:

> 'So what you're saying is . . .?'

> 'Would I be right that you think . . .?'

Because words mean different things to different people, it's wise to check.

> 'She's prevaricating.'
> 'Do you mean she's putting things off or that she's lying?'
> 'She's definitely stalling.'

> 'I'm determined to go on being celibate.'
> 'Do you mean you'll not have sex – or that you won't marry?'
> 'Give up sex, of course.'

(Incidentally, in those last two examples, the English language was the sufferer.)

Beginners must get into the habit of asking clarification questions. It is far too easy to misunderstand what is being said as a result of mishearings, wrong constructions, different ways of thinking, vocabulary being used differently by different age groups (e.g. 'It's wicked . . .').

Good open questions catch the interviewee's interest and unlock a wealth of information and opinion, encouraging them to talk freely because the interviewer appears interested in their views. The difficulty is that the interviewee may talk too much and swerve off on an unwelcome tangent, which is why for most interviews making it clear up front what you are after is so important.

Leading

Because they can usually be answered shortly, leading questions could be categorised as a subsection of closed questions.

> 'You're a Lib Dem, aren't you?'
>
> 'How did you react? Were you furious?'
>
> 'How much money went missing – more than £250,000?'
>
> 'Did the accident happen just after they left the pub?'

Leading questions have a bad reputation, yet they're much used in everyday conversation, and experience shows that if the interviewee likes the questioner, they have little effect on the answers unless the suggested answer is way off-beam.

Much more annoying can be the *assumptive* sub-category of leading questions, as in 'When did you stop beating your wife?'.

> 'Are you married or single?'
> 'Neither, I'm divorced!'
>
> 'Did you come by bus or train?'
> 'I walked.'

But, as before, if the assumption is correct these questions work well because they demonstrate understanding and interest.

> 'You love the sea.'
> 'Yes – with a passion. What made you say that?'
> 'That photo of the yacht on your bookcase.'
>
> 'I've heard you love opera – I guess Verdi in particular.'
> 'Yes – how did you know?'
> 'Just a feeling.'

This last comment may be because everything said so far showed an interest in the workings of the human heart – perhaps it was in the cuttings.

Sometimes, during very tricky interviews, using an assumptive question is one way to provoke an answer.

> 'When was the last time you smoked a joint?'

Asking an assumptive question that relates back to something said at an earlier stage of the interview can flatter the interviewee, reinforcing how interesting you find what they're telling you. Referring back and getting it wrong can lead to a complicated and useful correction, but don't try this too often or they may suspect you're not as shrewd as they first thought.

> 'So when you said earlier that the samples taken from the reservoir passed all the required tests, that means the water quality has been maintained at the same standard since the reservoir was built?'
>
> 'No, no – you can't assume that. The test standards were lowered some years back. Take, for example, the requirements for testing for *e. coli* . . .'

Indirect assumptive

Indirect assumptive questions are useful when you need to overcome a barrier. Best known is the classic:

> 'How many raffle tickets would you like?'

. . . instead of:

> 'Would you like any raffle tickets?'

So:

> 'How many redundancies will there be?'

Not:

> 'Will there be any redundancies?'

Lastly, there's a *leading question* variation which demands a Yes/No reply – when either reply could land the interviewee in difficulties. This has been called a 'classic conflict' question and is used most viciously on politicians, who hate to be seen or heard squirming to avoid a straight answer. For an example, see page 121.

Directive, suggestive or loaded

These questions are unattractive and manipulative, not recommended, but regularly used by unfortunate journalists who have to return with quotes to fit a pre-set formula, slot into a known space or support a management opinion.

> 'You're happy to feed your child Frankenstein foods, not knowing what appalling deformities might result in years to come?'
>
> 'It's undeniable that 20mph zones save lives, so why should selfish, speeding motorists be listened to?'
>
> 'Mother Teresa [the Pope, the Prime Minister . . .] said love was the most important thing in the universe. Don't you agree?'
>
> 'What sort of mother wouldn't support our campaign to have the names and addresses of local paedophiles published?'

Short, simple, clear

Since the first interview requirement is to communicate, commonsense dictates that short questions are better than long ones, simple questions better than convoluted ones, clear questions better than abstruse ones. Commonsense may dictate this but, alas, commonsense is a rare commodity. This is where using a recorder and listening back to interviews is embarrassingly instructive.

When it comes to broad or narrow, objective or subjective questions, there can be no pat answer. The guideline is to make the question relevant to your requirements and to the personality of the interviewee.

Cautious, legalistic minds dislike broad questions.

> 'What did you think of Australia?'
> 'In what way? Do you want to know my reaction to the people, the scenery, the wine, what exactly?'

The more relaxed and less exact would have no such worries with the same question.

> 'Wonderful place. Loved it, especially crossing the Nullabor plain by train, fireworks in Sydney on New Year's Eve, kangaroos and parrots on the golf course. And the natives were friendly – especially when Australia were beating us at cricket.'

If you're after a lot of information, move carefully from broad-brush to detailed follow-ups, particularly if the interviewee is at all wary. Long, complicated follow-up questions immediately after a broad general question signal that there's a lot of very detailed questioning to follow, and if time is short and you are less than endearing, the interview may end swiftly. Consider this scenario:

> 'Have you ever lived in Cambodia?'
> 'Yes. For six months, really loved it.'

There follows a long list of questions requiring detailed information about the standard of accommodation, food, transport, trains, weather, shops. All are answered patiently.

> 'Have you ever lived in Laos?'
> 'Yes. For two months . . .'

Same long list of questions follow. Interviewee is less patient.

> 'Have you lived in China?'
> 'No.'
> 'Or Thailand?'
> 'Never!'

The advice is to ask all your general questions first, then go back and obtain the details you want.

Customise your questions

Make your questions suit your interviewee. People who are at home with facts and figures, people who are well defended or pompous or tentative or scared, usually resist hypothetical questions. The creative, by contrast, welcome the 'what would you do if . . .?' approach and will freewheel away into fantasy, which can make for good copy.

More than that, make your questions exact and precise. Enthusiasm makes for good quotes, so if your research shows that your interviewee has a passion for quattrocento (fifteenth-century Italian) art, frame an exact question.

> 'If you had to choose one picture that sums up all you love about quattrocento art, which would it be – and why?'

Or if your interviewee is a noted vegetarian celebrity:

> 'If you were planning a gourmet vegetarian meal, what would you cook and who would you invite?'

Hopping between objective and subjective questions – queries about observable facts or happenings and about personal opinions and views – can be very disturbing for interviewees, particularly those who think exactly, logically and slowly. Only the disorganised and/or creative can cope with fanciful queries.

Avoid interrogation

There's a school of interviewing that recommends interviewers should adopt a variety of stances, from investigator and confessor to inquisitor and judge. But investigators often operate under cover, confessors behind a screen, inquisitors have recourse to torture, and judges require people to be on oath.

In other words, unless it's absolutely necessary, don't. Always try to interview person-to-person, adult-to-adult, eyeball-to-eyeball. Neither abase nor elevate yourself, unless your interviewee will not talk otherwise. In these egalitarian days, being condescended to is appalling and being venerated wearying.

Interviewers who see themselves as attorneys for the public, intimidating and cross-examining their interviewees into a state of gibbering incoherence, do nothing for journalism, according to Anthony Howard in *The Times*. Interviewers who soothe have much more success. 'A good bedside manner', says Howard, 'is still the best way to elicit a scoop.'

Beguile not browbeat

Brilliant writer Clive James believes that the adversarial style is . . .

> . . . pretty nearly useless even when you interview a real adversary. If I had asked Ronald Reagan 'Were you a stoolie for the FBI in Hollywood?' he would have told me nothing. I asked him 'How serious *was* the Communist threat in Hollywood?' and he told me everything, implicating himself up to the eyebrows.

One of the most beguiling interviewers I ever watched at work was on the staff of an obscure trade publication. Interviewees said that being interviewed by him was like being wrapped in a fur bedspread – soft, silky and strangely seductive. They felt compelled to answer his questions because they sensed it mattered so much to him.

If you're interviewing on a sensitive subject – money, sex, relationships, education (never forget that, to many people, their lack of qualifications is a very sensitive matter indeed) – do not be embarrassed or judgemental. That sends out all the wrong messages, and your interviewees will sense your attitude and in turn feel embarrassed or furious. Be straightforward, don't use euphemisms, avoid judgemental words. No questions involving 'unconventional tendencies', 'surprising impulses' or 'facing up to problems'. Be matter-of-fact.

Every journalist I've met who has done a sex interview began by thinking it would be difficult and discovered the only problem was shutting the interviewee up. You usually learn more than you expect, sometimes more than you wish. Interviewing the vulnerable is a very different matter, requiring a different approach (see pages 172–77).

Telling trio

You need only three questions, it's said. The composer Brahms said they were: 'Whence? Wherefor? Whither?' A TV reporter said that for TV it was 'How bad is it? Is it getting worse? What can be done?'

A newspaper version is: 'When did this start? And then? What of the future?' These are all, in effect, questions to discover the beginning, the middle and the end of a story – the basis of so much journalism.

So when trying to find out the beginning, middle and end of the story, remember that what's needed is a mix of your keenness to listen to what they have to say and the quality and freshness of your questions.

For a charity promotion, journalists interviewed a man who planned to walk all round the British coast. When would he set off, they asked; what was his route; how long would it take; where would he stay; how much would he raise for charity – all routine stuff that he'd answered many times before. Then someone asked: 'What about your *feet*?' And at that point he perked up, the pack perked up, and the story took off.

Useful questions

Here's a selection of questions that have worked for a variety of journalists. There are no such things as never-fail questions, because so much depends on how they're asked and who asks them – but there are some reliables if used when appropriate. These include old faithfuls such as:

> 'What's the best/worst . . . ?'
>
> 'If you had two minutes on national TV . . .'
>
> 'Who's been the greatest influence on you?'
>
> 'Do you have a pet hate?'

Part of the function of a book such as this one is to offer examples of different questions for consideration, but please, when you interview, ask questions in your own words – otherwise you'll be like the unfortunate salespeople who have to work from a script: not happy, not convincing, and not very successful.

To an interviewee speaking in jargon:

> 'How would you explain that to a lay person?'

For any successful person:

> 'Have you any advice for youngsters just setting out?'

For business or political interviews where you've just heard a controversial opinion and/or inflated claim:

> 'What evidence do you have for that?'

If you meet someone on a factory visit, at a press conference, visiting a local organisation, and you can't remember their name:

> 'Remind me how you spell your name again.'

For a high-flying businessperson:

> 'How come you, of all the company's 10,000 [or however many] employees, made it to the top?'

For people still climbing the ladder:

> 'What drives/motivates you?'

There is a remarkable set of questions devised by Eric Berne, author of *Games People Play*, in his book *What Do You Say After You Say Hello?* They link in with the parent/adult/child approach of transactional analysis. Here's a selection:

'What will it say on the front of your tombstone?'

'If your family were put on the stage, what sort of play would it be?'

'What did your parents forbid you to do?'

'Do you ever lie awake at night planning revenge?'

'How far ahead do you begin to worry about things?'

'What will your last words be?'

A variation on that approach is to ask

'If you *had* to find a needle in a haystack, how would you do it?'

Answers to this last question are said to reveal the root of your being:

'Hire someone to do it for me,' said an economist.

'Burn it down and use a metal detector,' said a powerful businessman.

'Use a giant magnet,' said a playwright.

Here's a set of hypothetical questions to ask an articulate interviewee who's in rare form:

You meet a man at the end of the world and he asks you three questions which you have to answer spontaneously and immediately. The first is: 'Who are you?'
[Pause for answer]
The second question is: 'Apart from that who are you?'
[Pause for answer]
And the last is: 'Apart from *that* who are you?'

Suppose your interviewee shows signs of wanting to go and you're sure there's much more to come:

'Am I boring you?'

. . . said to guarantee another 20 extra minutes.

To an interviewee who refuses to give a direct answer to a pointed question and squirms around, fudging his or her replies:

'I'll take it that's a yes.'

Almost every newspaper or magazine Q&A feature has some questions that can be used for a general profile interview.

> 'What books are on your bedside table?'
>
> 'What really pisses you off?'
>
> 'If you could make one change to the world/your company/your town/village/club – with money no object – what would it be?'
>
> 'What's your motto?'
>
> 'Where do you expect to be in five years' time?'
>
> 'How do you handle disappointment?'
>
> 'What makes you feel important?'
>
> 'What's the most important lesson you've learned in life?'
>
> 'Who's your hero?'
>
> 'What three words would you use to describe yourself?'
>
> 'If you were a biscuit, what sort would you be?'
>
> 'If you knew you were going to die tomorrow, what would you do tonight?'

Softly, softly

Skilful interviewers can ask almost anybody anything and get a reasonable response. Approach and style are what count. You can ask tough or rude questions if you ask them in the right way.

You need to be seen as sympathetic and understanding by the person you're talking to. They must feel they can trust you. Robert McCrum, when literary editor of the *Observer*, was a 'Desert Island Discs' castaway and wrote a feature about it, which captures a central point about being interviewed. 'I would happily', he wrote, 'have spent all day discussing the infinitely fascinating subject of Me.'

The really offensive questions are those that relate to what people can't change – their height, the colour of their skin, physical abnormalities. But even those can be asked sympathetically once the interview is under way. Lynda Lee-Potter, First Lady of Fleet Street, once waited 45 minutes before asking an interviewee if she took her artificial leg off at night. When Lee-Potter judged the time was right, she received a slightly puzzled answer: 'Yes, of course.'

Start nice . . .

If you want to ask important questions that you sense your interviewee will not wish to answer, approach gently and, if you meet refusal, anger or aggression, quickly veer away – apologising if that's your style – and return to the subject later.

If you want to ask questions that you *know* will cause trouble, commonsense may dictate that you leave them until the end when you have the bulk of the interview in the bank. Then, if thrown out, you can still write the story.

However, commonsense can be wrong. Much depends on how the interviewee is likely to react and whether it's *a* tough question or *the* tough question. (To see how talented journalists Lynn Barber, Emma Brockes, Andrew Duncan and Jan Masters face such problems relating to celebrities, go to pages 144–64.)

Warn of a change of tack

With a few exceptions – for example, people you are trying to wrongfoot or trap – the best way to ask an unpleasant question is to give fair warning. You tell your interviewee you are going to ask a difficult/hard/rude/impertinent/offensive question and then you do. Because they are prepared, the sting goes out of the question and they feel more able – and more obliged – to answer. Try it.

> 'I know it's daft, but journalists always have to put the age in – so how old are you?'
>
> 'This may be really offensive, but why – when you work in such a sober business – do you wear such cheesy ties?'
>
> 'I know you're important and run a department with a budget of several millions, but why did you put your feet on the desk just now?'

> 'This may sound rude, but you're 45, a mother of four and working with people whose lives are wrecked – so why the *Star Trek* watch?'

> 'This may be too difficult to answer – but how come such a disorganised person as you managed to edit a dictionary?'

Other approaches with difficult questions

First: make the question very simple. This is highly recommended for well-protected, skilled and tricky interviewees.

> 'Will you explain why you are not implementing your planned factory expansion?'

No criticism, no loaded words, no added details, no named sources for the interviewee to latch on to and attack. This approach makes it difficult for interviewees to dodge, divert or rubbish the question.

Second: lay the blame elsewhere.

> 'Your detractors say your company has a reputation for going in for cartels, tax avoidance – things people think multinationals shouldn't do. Do you think that's fair criticism?'

This allows you to ask a tough question but offers your interviewee the chance to see it as enabling them to counter hostile allegations.

Third: soften with schmooze – preface the attack with praise.

> 'Your latest movie has won five Oscar nominations and is doing great business at the box office – but isn't the bidet scene really tacky?'

Fourth: treat it lightly by implying the question is not so serious.

> 'I'd like to play devil's advocate here and look at what you did from a different angle. Then the question becomes – why did you put your name forward, considering your track record?'

Fifth: try separate apparently disconnected questions – a two-step approach.

> 'You've always been idealistic, haven't you? I know you support animal welfare charities and would never wear fur. I'm right there, aren't I?'

You already know the answer to these two questions, so you then follow them up with:

> 'So why do you send your children to a fee-paying school when you believe in equality of opportunity?'

Good humour, humour and cheek

Good humour in an interviewer is a great plus unless your interviewee is pompously self-important. A cheerful approach helps interviewees relax. It also can prevent and/or defuse anger, deflect aggression and lighten intense situations.

In most interviews, humour works wonders. No book can help you here; you're on your own. But if you've got the ability to make people laugh, use it. Amid the serious business of information extraction, making a cheeky comment is the equivalent of a feint in judo. It changes the dynamics and gives you the initiative.

Another plus. If you make your interviewee laugh, you move out of the questioning slot. Two provisos: know your own deficiencies – not everyone can tell a joke or an anecdote successfully. Second, ensure your interviewee is laughing with you.

Flattery

It's deeply worrying how much flattery people can absorb. It rarely goes amiss, because it makes them feel valued, reassures them all is well and with luck gets them to drop their defences.

Sincere compliments are the best. Kind remarks are better than nothing. There's usually something you can find to praise or at the least comment on positively.

> 'Great book – particularly the part . . .'

If the interviewee has written a book, you must read it if you have time, or – if time is short – at least know something more about it than the title.

> 'You always give me such lively, vivid quotes.'

Try this even if their quotes are not amazingly outstanding, because one of the great things about people is that performance regularly rises to meet expectations.

> 'Someone who's gone as far as you in such a short time is an inspiration.'
>
> 'What a speech!'

Most people who work in the public gaze, from film stars and actors to novelists and celebrity chefs, crave reassurance. Publicity is important to them so they look for a warm reception. Silence sends out the wrong vibes. The advice is: if you can say something flattering, do; if you can't, then keep quiet – but whatever you do, keep hostile thoughts to yourself. Barry Norman, who worked on the *Daily Mail* for many years, says that you start from the understanding that most stars are acutely conscious of the thrusting young talent in the wings, eager to displace them.

When you need more ...

So far, we've been in that happy land where interviewees gladly respond. Their answers may be incomplete or unclear, but under extra questioning they give vivid instances and lively anecdotes and expand incomplete replies, providing in full the answers you seek. They're neither monosyllabic nor gabby, neither evasive nor hostile.

Sadly, as everyone discovers, interviews aren't always like that.

What if your approach has been faultless and your questions good, yet you're disappointed with the quality or amount of information provided? We now shift up a gear to techniques to use on those who give less than you want, don't give or are evasive or reluctant to answer. These ploys come in no order of efficacy – success depends on skilful use in the right hands with responsive interviewees.

Nor do the techniques come with a guarantee. News management is now so sophisticated that journalists must accept that, on occasion, they won't win. That doesn't mean you should capitulate – though it may mean you should appear to capitulate. You can choose any one of these strategies:

- Persist
- Keep them talking
- Suggest/guess
- Hint at dissatisfaction
- Wheedle and needle
- Threaten 'no comment'
- Float a rumour
- Play 'grandmother's footsteps'
- Get tough
- Tell a story
- Offer a confidence.

Persist with questioning

If your interviewee doesn't want to answer, you may decide to move onto the next subject. That is tantamount to admitting defeat unless you do so deliberately, intending to return to the subject later. You're there to get the interview, so ask the question again, maybe in a softer or more oblique form, maybe more forcefully. Tell them this is a valuable opportunity to set the record straight, dispel rumours, put their side of the story. Try any ploy you feel comfortable with.

'So the question's too hard for you?' may not suit everyone, but if said jokingly it can ease the tension, which is sometimes all it takes. If they continue to refuse to answer, move on but return and ask it again later.

Keep them talking

Keep your cool, keep your head, and keep them talking. The more they talk, the more noticeable refusals are.

I once interviewed a man who insisted on seeing the questions in advance. He was six months into a very difficult and newly created job, had attracted a lot of flak and had previously refused to talk. Reluctantly I sent over 20 questions, was given an hour, and was told by his secretary that he'd be all right if I could make him laugh.

After the preliminaries, I started on my questions. He refused point blank to answer the first six, all about sales and market share. An inauspicious start. I changed tack and we started to talk in general terms. We both relaxed a little, and he did start to laugh. By the end of 45 minutes he was chatting away openly and volubly about what a success the company was, so I chanced it: 'C'mon, all's going well, you're surely not going to hide your successes. Just tell me . . .'

And he did. None of the figures was accurate, I am certain – he left not too long after – but, 'sourced', they made interesting reading. My belief is that he'd disclosed too much to withdraw at the critical point, realising how damaging it would look. I listened again to that tape a lot, and it's possible to hear his voice drop and change tone as he begins to give the highly suspect figures (see pages 80–1).

Suggest/guess

This is the simplest and often the most effective way of coping with reluctance about statistics.

> 'We're spending more than a quarter of a million.'
> 'Would that be more than £300K or more than £400K?'

It depends how practised your interviewees are. If they say 'Yes', then another figure will be suggested.

> 'More than half a million?'

Suppose they reply:

> 'We'd rather not discuss the actual budget.'

Then a comeback could be:

> 'Would between . . . and . . . be a safe bet?'

Again, if they reply 'Yes', you can go on narrowing down until either you get to a printable answer or they pull out. After a second blunt refusal it is best to give up. You can always refer to the refusal to answer in your copy.

There are occasions when a grossly improbable guess may give you a clue about how near you are, as people tend to deny wild improbabilities more fervently than close-to-the-mark guesses. Watching body language can help gauge any response (see pages 71–77).

Hint at dissatisfaction

One way to encourage your interviewee to give more is to get your disappointment across. First, the (slightly more) subtle approach. If you're using a notebook and pen, quietly put the cap back on the pen or close the notebook. I discovered this by chance when interviewing the manager of Pebble Beach Country Club, near to San Francisco:

> We'd had a very good interview indeed. 'How much do you earn?' I asked at one point and he told me – a rare occurrence but always worth trying.
>
> He was a lively talker with some great stories but in effect we'd descended to chitchat after lunch, so I closed my notebook and had noticed him watching me. A minute or two later he said something so quote-worthy I had to open the book again. The reasoning is simple. I'd been hanging on his words appreciatively – very good for his ego – then had noticeably switched off. He realised he could get more attention and applause, so started to give again.

The more cruel version is to switch off the recorder.

When time is short and you can't afford to close your notebook or turn off the recorder, then either blame the editor, the features editor, yourself or – last resort – them; but in a kindly way:

> 'This isn't working. I'm obviously asking the wrong questions. Can we start again?'
>
> 'The editor's setting great store by this interview. She'll give me hell if I don't get something meatier.'
>
> 'I'd hoped for something sexier. You've always been so quotable before.'
>
> 'I'd hoped you would give me something stronger.'
>
> 'I hate to say this, but I think the editor's going to say this is all a little predictable.'
>
> 'I'm back on writing wedding captions if I don't get some really powerful quotes – so *please*!'

Wheedle and needle

Plead or prod. Not everyone can – or would want to – do this; but it's very effective when practised by a skilled interviewer.

> 'Oh, come on, you can tell me . . .'
>
> 'Why won't you say? Oh, please . . .'
>
> 'You're not too afraid to tell, surely?'
>
> 'Question too hard, I guess.'

Threaten 'no comment'

If your interviewee refuses to answer a particular question, one approach is to point out how bad that will look in print. A lot depends on the reputation of your publication. The higher it's rated, the worse an omission looks. This ploy works better on the inexperienced interviewee. Always worth a try.

Float a rumour

This is an insider variation on the 'suggest-an-answer' tactic, requiring the ground to be prepared carefully beforehand. It goes this way. A journalist wants to find out how the fashion chain's business is going after a mammoth expansion, but no one will say. They ask the chief executive:

> 'What's this I hear about the downturn in takings in your West Midlands operation?'
>
> 'What? Where did you hear this?'
>
> 'On the grapevine.'

If on one or two previous occasions the journalist has presented a real tip this way, the chief executive should have developed a healthy respect for their sources and – the hope is – should either spill the beans or deny everything on the record. It does work, I can vouch for that. However, if you overdo it – like so much in journalism – you'll be sussed.

Play 'grandmother's footsteps'

This requires great delicacy. Having established what your interviewee does not want to talk about, you creep up on the subject again and again from all angles, veering away at the last minute. They've already signalled that they're unhappy to talk about it and, if you're a skilled practitioner, you can really rattle them so that in the end – the theory goes – they're relieved to be able to discuss it. This requires confidence and skill (see Andrew Duncan on pages 150–5).

Get tough

The ground rules of interviewing are to be sceptical, not adversarial, and never to antagonise interviewees. Break these rules at your peril. However, with a particularly frustrating interviewee who has resisted every gambit you know and who you can afford to antagonise, you might consider a hostile question. But ask it with a smile and never lose your temper. If all else fails, insult them – but only if you never need to talk to them again.

Tell a story

A good anecdote will tell readers more about a person than any amount of description. To encourage the interviewee to provide one, remind them of a previous anecdote you found in the cuttings. They may be delighted to retell it with advantage, or – even better – come out with a lively new one.

Offer a confidence

This isn't as creepy as it sounds when done unintentionally. Done deliberately, it can appear tacky, but it can work – though not always.

For example, take this instance. Interviewer and interviewee (a novelist) are getting along well, and common ground had been established – they've discovered they have both just ended a long-term relationship, and they're both addicted to chocolate.

The novel in question contains vivid sex scenes, and is strong on anxiety about what can be transmitted. The interviewer can't resist saying:

> 'I got thrush once and had to visit an STD [Sexually Transmitted Diseases] clinic. At first I was terrified but ended up quite fancying the consultant.'
>
> 'That's astonishing,' replies the novelist. 'It happened to me, too.'

There's a pause. The novelist is asking herself which person's embarrassing experience is likely to end up in print.

Questions *not* to ask

- Don't ask what you should already know from research.
- Don't ask the first question that leaps to your mind. It will have leapt to every other mind, too.
- Don't prove how stupid you are by asking smart-arse, clever-clever questions. They infuriate interviewees (a) because they break the important 'they're-the-star' guideline, and (b) because you're showing off rather than trying to gather information.
- Don't badger or hector. It's counter-productive.
- Above all, don't – OK, very, very rarely – ask: 'How do you feel?'

> 'Your mother's been eaten by a crocodile, your father's been electrocuted, and your husband's gone missing in Borneo. How do you feel?'

People who want to tell you how they feel won't need this question to prompt them, and people who can't put their feelings into words won't need it either. One way of putting it that has been known to work is to ask: 'What did that do to you?'

Ploys *not* to fall for

Beware if you're asked for your opinion. This is an experienced interviewee's way of flattering you, getting you on their side and so stopping probing assessments. The interviewee is turning the tables: using a successful interviewing ploy on you (see page 171).

'Tell me about you . . .'

Shrewd, manipulative or very nice interviewees may ask you questions about yourself. Deflect these immediately. Lynn Barber recounts how at one point the actress Julie Andrews asked her if she had any children. She has two daughters, but said she had none, because she knew that being a pleasant woman, Andrews would ask about them and she didn't want to divert or break up the flow of the interview.

CASE STUDY 3 – DON'T DESPAIR

What do you do when all your efforts to gather good copy have come to nothing? Here's how a talented feature writer remembers one of her early jobs.

> The dullest newspaper I ever worked for was dead keen on accuracy and getting the facts right, which was good training, but it was rather uninterested in anything vaguely stylistic. If you didn't start with 'A local woman/man/boy aged something or other . . .', the subs put it up front anyhow.
>
> The paper covered everything – including listing all the people (with names and addresses checked on the electoral registers, telephone book, etc.) who had been prosecuted for not having a television licence or parking on the wrong side of the road.
>
> One of the regular chores was interviewing anybody who had enough years of service with the railway or the local car manufacturer. The effort needed to make each one just a little different was immense. One day I went with a photographer on such a job and found my interviewee very heavy weather indeed. I despaired of getting a single spark to lighten up this routine news item and had got up to go when I noticed on the wall a photograph of a ship.
>
> 'Oh, were you a sailor?' I asked. 'Yes,' he said. 'I was shipwrecked three times.'
>
> I nearly missed the best retirement story I ever covered.

What if they're reluctant?

This is something that happened a long time ago, but it embodies a truth as valuable now as it was then.

Diana Menuhin, the wife of the violinist Yehudi, who was giving recitals throughout Australasia, reluctantly agreed to spare *Auckland Star* reporter Ann Elder about 10 minutes.

Ann arrived with a photographer. For a start, Mrs Menuhin refused to have her picture taken – yet a few minutes later she was being photographed in the street, smiling, wearing her new Pierre Cardin trouser-suit and carrying a brown paper bag full of health food. The subsequent interview was meant to last for just 10 minutes. Two hours later Ann and Diana were still talking.

Why the change? Because of the practised persuasion of Harold Paton, one of New Zealand's top photographers, and the determination of a reporter not to let the interview slip through her fingers.

Mrs Menuhin had started by saying to the photographer: 'No photo . . . when you've had looks and lost them . . .', but he was genuinely complimentary and obviously very keen to photograph her. Such subtle flattery is hard to resist.

She later talked at length to Ann in the hotel room while doing the ironing. Why? Because Ann knew a great deal about ballet, and remembered that in her youth Diana Menuhin had danced with a very famous company – and that connection opened the floodgates of memory.

The message to us all is: 'Never take no for an answer.' Photographers are particularly persuasive because their opportunity is limited; if they don't get the pic there and then, the opportunity will probably have passed for good. Phones and emails make it easier for writers.

5
Understanding interviewees and avoiding problems

Body language

We speak with our voices but communicate with our whole bodies. Not an original idea, but one sometimes dismissed by word-oriented journalists. Trainers, who watch a lot of interviews, become body language converts. They observe an aggressive posture adopted by the interviewer and see how it puts an interviewee on the defensive. They recognise from a cluster of movements that the question just asked has hit a target that the interviewee is unwilling to discuss.

Interviewees, primarily concerned with their responses, know how they felt about the question or the interviewer. Often, after watching a recording of the interview, they understand how the question or the questioner's body language affected them, or see how their body language showed what they were feeling.

Journalists, particularly beginners, are much harder to convince, probably because they're tuned to what's said and getting that down accurately – so much so that, at first, they are deaf to the subtleties of body language.

Body language is not an *exact* science. Folded arms may mean that interviewees feel defensive or that they sit that way because they find it comfortable, though that in itself shows something about them. Shifts in posture become significant and worth noting when an interviewee who has been leaning forward and talking freely, suddenly leans back and folds their arms. Something caused the change, most likely what was being talked about at that time. That *is* worth following up.

The most important aspects for interviewers are:

- Appearance
- Eyes
- Face
- Gestures
- Head
- Posture.

A quick look at various aspects of body language follows. Readers who want to learn more about this rewarding skill – a lot of them, I trust – should look at *The Definitive Book of Body Language* by Allan and Barbara Pease, which lives up to all that the title promises (see page 235).

Appearance

This conveys the most immediate impression, but it is also the one that can most easily be changed. Chewed fingernails can be covered with false ones. Expensive accessories such as an Anya Hindmarch handbag can add lustre to (though not disguise) a Marks & Sparks trouser suit. An expensive haircut can transform a person's looks.

Though appearance makes an immediate impact, a warm engaging character soon means that weird clothes, down-at-heel shoes or chewed fingernails move down the ratings ladder. As one ugly charmer said: 'Give me five minutes with them and they'll forget the face.'

That aside, what interviewees look like does tell you something. Beards and spectacles are often used as protection, as distancing. It's well known that overweight men with beards often shave them off once they have shed a lot of weight. The chairman of a famous aviation company told a *Financial Times* reporter that he wore a beard because it saved him 10 minutes a day in shaving time, which built to an hour a week, five whole days a year.

Experienced fraud investigator Mike Comer, Director of Cobasco Group Ltd, says he looks for inconsistencies: 'a reasonably average suit paired with perhaps a gold Rolex watch'. He's particularly suspicious of men with fancy footwear – crocodile skin, buckles, tassels, silk socks. 'I think most of the crooks I've dealt with have had some hang-up with their feet.'

Eyes

You have to look at the person you're interviewing, the only exceptions being when you're making notes, checking your questions or perhaps encouraging confessions (see page 175). Don't drop your eyes when your interviewee looks at you. This is a signal that you're not enjoying their company, but don't read the same into their eye movements. Interviewees look away while talking, particularly if recalling incidents and anecdotes. However, people who talk to you with their eyes closed may either be bored or feel superior; either way they don't feel like eyeballing you.

Continued eye contact while listening indicates approval, encouragement and positive feedback. The more people look at each other, the more they grow to like each other. It's staring that makes people uncomfortable, since starers are seen as dominant.

Once you are confident about meeting interviewees, you might start to watch which way their eyes flick when they break after first contact. This could give some indication whether they tend to be artistic with good visual imagination (break to their left), or scientific (to their right).

You can test this yourself with a colleague. Sit so that you can observe their eye movements clearly and ask them to think about their bedroom when they were eight. Odds are that they will look up and to their left. Ask them what features they'd most like in a new kitchen, and odds are they will look up to their right. Ask them to remember what was the last thing said to them at work the previous day, and odds are they will look to their left. Ask them to think what they'd like to say if they had two minutes on TV and they may look to their right.

Ask them to think about the rules of football and they may well look down to their left. Ask about their feelings on capital punishment, and they may well look down to their right. The theory is that people look upwards when recalling or constructing images; on the level when they're remembering what's been said or trying to put things into words; and downwards when recalling feelings or having an internal dialogue.

All this may be of no use to you in an interview, but you never know. Some investigative journalists certainly use it as an indicator of whether an actual (truthful) location or image is being remembered (up and left) or an invented one (up and right).

Lying is covered on pages 77–81. Here, it's enough to say that if an interviewee's eyes flick quickly away before answering a key question, ask it again or later in another way and watch their body language very carefully.

Face

People's faces can register all sorts of emotions – fear, happiness, misery, anger, surprise, contempt – but do so more rarely during an interview, as most people learn to control their expressions to some extent.

Experienced interviewees, business people particularly, are good at this, though occasionally the mask slips and there's a fleeting glimpse of anger at a particularly annoying question. The skill is to watch for changes of expression – maybe from interested listening to a cold smile. Why? Or from a real smile to tightened lips and jaw. Again, why?

Gestures

Hand signals have a bewildering variety of meanings. For interviewers there are a number of 'signals' that merit a mention:

- Steepling, where the hands are in a prayer-like position with fingertips together but palms apart, is said to show seniority, superiority, confidence.
- Index finger-wagging often reveals a bullying 'I know best' temperament. Some interpreters say the finger represents a Neanderthal club.
- Ticking off points on the fingers of one hand with the forefinger of another, 'One, two, three . . .' is said to (and probably does) show an authoritarian nature.
- Twirling a pair of spectacles round and round mimics the TV 'wind-up-soon' hand signal – and means the same in my experience.
- Pushing real or imaginary items away with the hands and picking or flicking imaginary fluff off clothes is often interpreted as dismissing or rejecting what is being heard, be it question or suggestion.

- A hand near the mouth is often interpreted as a pale echo of the hand involuntarily clapped over the mouth after some appalling indiscretion, suggesting anxiety or even deception. The same is sometimes said of hands near the nose and eyes.
- There's not much agreement about the significance of anything put into the mouth: some say it's for reassurance, some say it masks aggression.
- Hands near the chin are said to show thought.
- Rubbing the back of the neck is read as a sign of frustration – dealing with something or someone who's really 'a pain in the neck'.

The position of the palms when the hands are extended in a conversation can be telling. If an interviewee is trying to explain something to you and says: 'Look . . .', extending a hand, palm up, towards you, it's likely they are more affable than if the hand is extended palm down. Try it out yourself. Palms up equals acceptance; palms down negation.

Hand movements can provide the hand-mover with reassurance. Neck-stroking, mouth-touching movements are called 'pacifiers'. Interviewees suddenly exhibiting these may be trying to calm themselves down.

Arms can be used as a defence (crossed), a welcome (open) or to attack (thrust out). Legs can be uncrossed, splayed or crossed in a variety of ways, and much here depends on conditioning. Tightly crossed legs, legs crossed 'in parallel' or crossed legs tucked securely under a chair are all usually signs of nervousness, insecurity, withdrawal or lack of cooperation in both sexes.

Men who sit with their legs wide apart are said to be 'displaying', sending out a sexual message. If they sit with one foot resting on the other knee, the 'figure four' position, this is interpreted as being relaxed and open. It's more common in North America than Europe. It's impossible to generalise with women: some are trained to cross their ankles but never their legs, others never to sit cross-legged at all. Most do what's comfortable.

The important thing about the crossing and uncrossing of legs is when it occurs. It happens for a number of reasons, obviously, but particularly when interviewees feel uncomfortable. You've only got to do a few interviews to realise the truth of this. The skilled interviewer needs to notice if this occurs at any significant point in the questioning.

At one smart press conference about corporate sponsorship, four captains of industry sat on a raised platform without the benefit of desk or table to shield them. The questioning was going well, until one journalist asked: 'What of the supposed influence of the chairman's wife in deciding what to sponsor?' Four pairs of legs were uncrossed and recrossed simultaneously. It made me realise why so many politicians feel happier behind a desk or table.

Feet and heads

Feet are the greatest giveaways. Just as twenty-first-century man still experiences a surge of adrenalin in a tight corner – the fight or flight response – so the feet of twenty-first-century interviewees still begin to shuffle or shift when they want to get away.

Feet are the hardest part of the body to control. If they suddenly start to tap or twitch, the interviewee isn't comfortable. If an interviewee turns and points their feet towards the exit, that small movement probably expresses a subconscious desire to leave.

Nods and head tilts signal encouragement and approval, so they're much more useful to the interviewer than the interviewee. What matters about the interviewee's head movements is how the head is carried: forward of the body looks rather aggressive; high generally gives an impression of superiority; dropped usually suggests depression or submission.

Posture

In a straightforward, uncomplicated interview an interviewee leaning forwards or towards you shows that everything is going well. You have engaged their interest and attention. If they are leaning away or backwards, they may either be very relaxed or have switched off and lost interest.

Leaning forward symmetrically, with both arms on the desk or tabletop, is said to indicate a more involved attitude than the asymmetrical lean – one arm resting on the arm of a chair, or the desk, which is said to show relaxation.

An interviewee's posture becomes harder to read in more complex interviews. They may be leaning away because you have just touched on something they do not wish to discuss.

Receive *and* send

One of the pluses of becoming proficient in reading body language is the realisation that you can use it to communicate with interviewees without their knowing.

- Lean towards the interviewee and they'll talk more, sensing that you like them.
- Nod and they'll carry on talking up to three or four times longer than otherwise. By contrast, refusing to nod can make an interviewee dry up.
- You want to interrupt? Lean forward and raise your head and hand slightly to gain their attention. Even better, lift a hand holding a pencil. Or try three fast nods; that can work, too. Slow nods encourage them to continue.
- They're talking too much? Cut back on the nods, lean back, look away and sigh softly or adopt a posture that is totally contradictory to theirs.
- You suspect they're telling lies? Cover your mouth or flick imaginary fluff from your jacket. If you catch their eye, look away for a second.

Because you get back very much what you send, it's important to sit comfortably, avoiding legs tightly twisted, crossed or clamped together. Badly done, attempts at control through body language will disturb your interviewee consciously or subconsciously. So practise first and be subtle.

Crazy – or just a phone call?

A great amount of 'instinctive' body language needs no translation because it means the same all round the world, but this doesn't apply to certain gestures which vary from country to country.

You may not need to know that twirling a forefinger on the temple doesn't indicate 'crazy' in Argentina but that 'you have a phone call'. But you should know that in Germany the same gesture of twirling a forefinger on a temple made by a motorist is so insulting to another motorist that people can be arrested for it.

It's also seriously important to know that in the Middle East the left hand is considered unclean and is reserved for 'bodily hygiene'. To quote from *Gestures: the Do's and Taboos of Body Language Around the World*: 'This custom is especially important to remember because . . . at communal dinners where food is often touched with the hands, the left hand should *never* be used for eating.'

And you should know that showing the sole of your shoe sends a rude message in many parts of the Middle and Far East. In Thailand, don't point your toes at people. There, the head is considered almost sacred and the foot is considered lowly and inferior.

Reacting

When John Lennon told Maureen Cleave that the Beatles were more famous than Jesus Christ, you can bet she *didn't* say: 'Wow! You really mean that? You can't be that big-headed!' No, it's a fair bet she nodded and listened, then asked another question before she made any notes. When the story was printed in the *Evening Standard* it caused a furore.

The moral – with very few exceptions – is don't let on if you're given a great quote. If you do, your interviewee may twig and backtrack or clam up, neither of which you want. However, this advice is dependent on what was said. For an outstanding example of a very talented writer who checked and double-checked when given one of the most amazing quotes ever, see page 23.

Lying

It's a trusting and naive journalist who thinks they are never lied to. The lies may be minor – the result of interviewees wanting to present themselves in a favourable light or because they want to fool the neighbours. They may even believe what they say at the time. On occasion, though, the lies are serious and designed to mislead: to bolster a company's share price, for example, or avoid prosecution. Sometimes lying is inevitable because it's necessary: cabinet reshuffles, for example, budget plans, company failures. Sometimes the lie is to protect reputations – the liar's or someone else's.

Sometimes the interviewee has forgotten the truth. It's established that the more you tell a lie, the more you accept it as the truth, until in the end you believe it. Sometimes the interviewee is passing on what they've been told, believing it to be true.

How journalists react when they suspect they're being lied to depends on who they're interviewing and who they're writing for. With some interviewees you can laugh and say 'Come off it, that can't be true . . .' With others, raise an eyebrow or smile mockingly. With others, nod sagely while remaining sceptical and come back to it later in the interview. Or appear deeply impressed but store it away for a later occasion. It's a judgement that only the interviewer can make.

Whatever the reason, lying matters – particularly in news and business stories. If someone lies, there's usually a story there.

It is very hard for most people to keep their eye movements under control while telling lies. People who have gazed steadily at you for the first 20 minutes of the interview may, quite involuntarily, blink more or glance away for a fraction of a second before telling a lie. But there's no one sure way to tell. For a start, good liars practise.

Good liars look you straight in the eye and speak up boldly, with no hesitation or telltale lowering or raising of the voice. Jonathan Aitken, an MP and later a government minister, regularly lied until he was brought down by a combination of *Guardian* journalists, Mohammed al-Fayed and his own pride – a story that ended with a prison sentence.

Clues

Some verbal and vocal clues to evasion or avoidance of the truth are easily recognisable and can be studied at leisure if you use a recorder. It's much more difficult if you use shorthand.

Easily recognisable clues include an immediate reluctance to answer, in full, in part or in any detail. For example, 'I can't tell you that . . . That's all I know . . .' It's always safer for someone avoiding the truth to say 'I can't remember' than to provide any detail. Be more inclined to accept a 'Can't remember' explanation if there's a pause before it's said, while the interviewee genuinely tries to recall.

If the interviewer challenges a 'Can't remember' answer, the interviewee may play for time by asking for clarification, countering with another question, answering an unasked question with contrived anger, extreme politeness or flattery, long rambling answers or emphatic repetition – 'Yes, yes, yes . . .' 'No, no, no . . .'.

Amateurs are the easiest to suss, and even then the indications are not foolproof; but there are guidelines to help. A company specialising in fraud detection worldwide, developed a checklist of visual, verbal and vocal clues that indicate when interviewees may be lying, but emphasise that there is no single response that can be judged conclusive. The checklist was devised after studying interviews designed specifically to establish the truth where, for example, evidence may be produced or previous answers questioned. Even so, it's valuable for investigative and business journalists.

It's estimated that managers are lied to on average about 30 times each week. An important distinction is made between good and bad lies, good being the 'I like your jacket' or 'wonderful meal' type of comment. Fraud estimator Mike Comer believes that the chances of most people detecting lies are no better than fifty-fifty. On average, he reports, police officers and psychiatrists score only slightly better. Interestingly, the most effective at detecting deceit was a group of criminals serving life sentences.

Comer says that it is possible for experienced interviewers, using a mixture of techniques, to achieve a much higher success rate if interviewees are judged on:

- The words they use and how they use them, such as:
  - quiet replies, when previously the interviewee has been speaking more loudly;
  - noticeably slower replies than those given previously.
- Their attitude.
- The emotions they display.
- Their body language.

Posture

Comer believes that posture is one of the most reliable visual giveaways. 'What you are looking for are significant changes in posture at times of significant questions.' These can be turning or leaning away from the interviewer, pushing the chair further back, getting up from a chair, or pushing away with the hands.

'People seldom lie to you "head on",' he says. 'They almost always sit at an oblique angle.' He sees any increased use of 'pacifier' hand movements as a subconscious reaction to feeling uncomfortable, and says that if someone who has been using a lot of hand movements to accompany what they're saying suddenly, at a key point in the interview, clasps their hands together, puts them in their pockets or behind their head, that's probably a good indication that they're hiding something. Comer believes that pauses before delivery can be another indicator of lying.

Foot movements are yet another. 'The further you are from the face, the nearer you are to the truth,' says one body language expert. Feet can also show boredom. Context determines which of the two it is.

Avoiding problems

Because interviewing is so complex, a lot can go wrong. Patently it's unwise to wear a 'Woman's Right to Choose' t-shirt when interviewing a pro-lifer. But who's to know that your interviewee has a pathological distrust of people who wear lime green, or detests the name Herbert, or loathes a Liverpool accent?

Taking avoiding action

First, recognise you're not going to get it right every time. You're bound to make mistakes, but practice does bring progress.

Aim to go into every interview as well prepared as possible. Recognise that many, if not most, of the people you interview early in your career may be both practised and skilled at getting their message across. You may come away thinking things went well when actually you've been neatly manoeuvred into writing at their behest. This is why planning is so important, why 'Know what you want to know' is one of the earliest injunctions. It's your best protection against being a sacrificial lamb, going all unknowing to the slaughter.

Many problems can be minimised by following some simple guidelines:

- Don't be in a hurry. It's insulting and demeans your interviewee's contribution. By all means tell them what time you have available, but during the interview don't rush or push them on in any way, except perhaps by giving them a warning when time is nearly up. If it's a face-to-face interview and you have to look at a watch, be sure it's theirs – *never* yours.

- Don't talk about yourself. This antagonises. They are the star of the interview. You are there to gather their thoughts, not contribute yours. The only time you should talk about yourself is in the very early rapport-building stage.
- Don't offer your own negative judgements.
- Don't ask long, convoluted questions.

It's also within your power to ensure you don't:

- make a poor impression when you phone them or walk through the door;
- phone or arrive underprepared and easy to fool;
- get behind in note-taking and miss a great quote;
- alienate them by an injudicious remark;
- let them take control;
- miss vital clues.

What can go wrong

Let's start with the most important.

You can let them take control

Dangerous. You will be told only what they want you to know, not what you want to find out. You might as well print a press release verbatim. Don't despair if it happens to you, just make sure it doesn't happen again. 'Catch me once, shame on you. Catch me twice, shame on me.'

If, as a beginner, you're caught this way, it will be because you're up against a well-trained interviewee, and the first thing they've been taught is to get down on their knees and thank God for a poorly prepared journalist. 'From a corporate view, journalists who ask vague questions are actually a huge advantage,' says a PR who trained executives from transnational companies. 'It means the executive can grab the agenda and say what they want to say.'

'No worries'

This PR trained executives in the ways of the press. They were encouraged not to be wary because in the past they had been misquoted; instead they should pre-empt this by arriving with their own agenda and ensuring that they got their message across. 'We teach interviewees to take control – and then they don't need to worry,' she said. Journalists, please note.

She spent considerable time enlightening her clients about the woolly heads of inept interviewers. They're not going to search through 30 recorded minutes looking for important messages, she said. 'You have to get your message across in the first three answers.' She trained clients who did eight half-hour face-to-face interviews in the afternoon with journalists who had sat through a presentation in the morning. She taught them to recognise the poor mutt who has lost the press release, hasn't read it, or else has but has already forgotten what it says. 'What staggers me,' she says . . .

> . . . is how many journallsts waste so much time wading back through the press release – proof that they're not thinking. With a good press release and a good press pack, you should be framing the story in your head and, when you get to interview the relevant executive, you should need around three or four quotes for the story – about 5 to 10 minutes – then the rest of the time you can get info for your next feature, sort out a facility visit, develop the relationship further.

The worst sin in her eyes? Wasting time going through company history when it's all on their website.

Executives are taught to 'word-bridge' or 'loop'. They learn that it doesn't matter what people ask because they don't treat the question as something that has to be answered literally.

> The question is an indication of a topic or area or belief or thought behind that question that you might choose to talk about. You can't do this unless you can create a bridge between something in the question and what you want to talk about. You're always going to bridge away from what you don't want to talk about.

Counter-ploys

What do journalists need to counter all this training? Every weapon in the armoury: training to understand what makes a story; the wit to work out what angle you're after; what information you need.

The PR rates honesty, too. 'Every time you admit you don't understand something, you win a thousand brownie points from the person you are interviewing. Most are more than willing to help you. What doesn't help is going "nod, nod, nod, yes of course," when you don't understand.'

She also rates curiosity and believes this draws out better responses than clever-clever questions designed to impress. Because she trained as a journalist, she admires skilled interviewers who know how to establish rapport, build trust and cope with bridging. Faced with these interviewers, her trained interviewees are on their guard. 'We warn them not to relax,' she says.

The journalists she admires arrive knowing what they want to know and are able to keep four story lines in their head, asking questions about each angle, mixing them up. This can puzzle or confuse an interviewee, which is very useful from the journalist's point of view because it deflects the interviewee from their pre-set agenda.

All good interviewers use the 'loop and circle' counter-ploy, neatly returning to points they want clarified, questions they want answered. Well done, it accumulates evidence, stacking up 'proof points', and slowly closes the net around the story.

Techniques to influence interviewees, covertly or overtly, include using body language (see page 77) and linguistic patterns. Such patterns 'take quite a bit of learning but they absolutely do work,' she says. Matching posture is the technique she rates highest, together with linguistic pattern mirroring.

The idea is that if someone says 'I see what you mean', the interviewer talks to them using visual words, but if they say 'I believe', the interviewer uses cognitive language.

You can alienate them

Make injudicious comments on what you're told and you could be in real trouble.

'I went to Jones Hill Academy but left last year.'
'I'm not surprised. It's an absolute dump, so my friends tell me. Deadhead tutors. Is Jim Smith – the one they call "Boredom Personified Smith" – still there?'
'Yes. Actually he's my uncle.'

'So when I was fired, to cheer myself up I went to see *Police Academy* and it really worked.'
'Yeah – great film! Didn't you love the Commandant's speech?'
'To be honest, I loathed it: puerile and disgusting. Walked out halfway through and bumped into an old friend who told me about a job going at ITN.'

'I have to go to North Wales tonight, but I'm not looking forward to it.'
'Yeah – nice country; shame about the people.'
'I'm going to my grandmother's funeral.'

You can bore them

You've got to make interviews interesting for your interviewee. Sometimes you'll be the twelfth person to have interviewed them that day. They'll be on auto-pilot and will wearily produce well-rehearsed answers unless you break the cycle with a fresh approach.

Probably the best way is to commiserate, to share the suffering; after all, you're both in a poor position. They're exhausted and you've drawn the short straw by going last. Use it to your advantage. By drawing attention to it, you show yourself in a sympathetic light, rather than just the latest in a long line of bloodsuckers, asking the same question – and so you put them on their mettle.

Give your questions a fresh twist and see if they can give you a fresh angle. You could even suggest opening the windows for some fresh air, or doing the interview walking round the block. Anything to break the monotony. See also Emma Brockes, page 148.

You can mishear

A local paper had to apologise. 'We are sorry we said the baby was found on a rubbish heap. This should have read "a rubber sheet".'

In an interview for *TVTimes* with a bestselling author, one journalist (me, actually) misheard 'bodice ripper' as 'body stripper'.

The *Guardian* quoted U2's Bono as saying 'I became a fan of club music, of *drug culture*, of everything that was going on at the time' – later correcting it to 'I became a fan of club music, of *club culture* . . .'.

Another *Guardian* correction:

> In our lead feature . . . about cannabis, we asked people whether they smoked it and quoted . . . Alex Salmond as saying: 'If you say "yes", people claim you're encouraging and supporting it, and if you say "no", it looks like you're a prick.' Mr Salmond has asked us to make it clear that what he actually said was 'prig' not 'prick'.

The moral is obvious. If the quote sounds at all unusual, or you're not sure you've heard correctly, query it, and never presume your interviewee uses the same language that you do.

You can misunderstand

Easily done. Your protection is total concentration, excellent research and a brain that hears, assesses and cross-checks information for consistency and sense.

> 'I've never been to Spain. The furthest south I've been is Parma.'
> 'But Palma's in Majorca, surely?'

You can lose the thread

You may feel it makes you look stupid to admit you don't understand what's being said, but you'll look far more stupid if you get it wrong in print.

You can show your hand

If you have an agenda you'd rather they didn't know about, don't make it clear from the very start by the thrust of your questions. Most political and business interviewees have considerable experience of the press, more than beginners realise, and subtlety is needed.

How to cope with difficult interviewees

What do you do when the trouble comes from your interviewees? How do you cope with the waffly, the evasive, the hostile and the monosyllabic? With charm, of course. With delicacy. And with deft firmness.

With the waffly and the evasive you take control, not by wrenching it back but by using the velvet choke chain operated by the iron hand. With the hostile and the monosyllabic you flip roles, slow down, vary your questions dramatically, become a shape-shifter, a changeling, a will-o'-the-wisp.

The wafflers

They may be nervous prattlers gushing out rubbish, or they may be egomaniacs in love with their opinions. Either way they talk too much and over-answer the question, adding, revising, rambling, diverging, sub-clausing, reminiscing . . . Stop! Rein them in. As always, honesty works best – but honesty of a subtle tint.

> 'What you say is amazing. I could listen all day, but I have to move us on. What about . . .'

The honesty here is partial but undeniable. Their waffle powers *are* amazing and you *could* listen all day – though you'd rather not. Note the 'move us on', kinder than 'move you on'. Go gently to the next question. If you're too brutal they will most likely clam up. They usually know they talk a lot, because friends will have told them.

Use all the body language devices to interrupt, of course (see page 77).

The evaders

More a velvet harness than a choke chain is needed here. Evaders slide off the subject with ease. One sentence they seem to be answering the question about enforcing the speed limit, and the next they're talking about how effective traffic calming measures can be and how cheap they are to install and, wow, you're off onto budgets.

A discussion about a big high street multiple's disappointing sales somehow turns into a conversation about the latest street fashions. Or questions about difficulties with software prompt details of an amazing new computer add-on. You've been 'looped' or 'word-bridged'. You should loop or word-bridge back.

> 'Fascinating, but what I really want to know is . . .'
>
> 'Wow, really – but first let's get back to . . .'
>
> 'That's a great story. I'd like to know much more – but first I'd like to clear up . . .'

Said smiling, and done with charm, this is a clear message that they've been sussed.

The hostile

These are the bullies, the aggressive bastards who power their way through regardless. Ask them a question they don't welcome and they go straight onto the attack. What they expect in return is aggression or submission.

Aggression they can cope with, because that's their speciality. They'll win here. Submission suits them fine, too. What they don't expect is amused surprise, a calm level gaze, a longish pause, concern for their blood pressure, a delighted 'that certainly hit home', or a tut-tutting 'dear me, we are upset . . . What *is* the matter?'

You must never be angry or hostile in return. If you lose your temper you lose the encounter. You have to force a change of pace, of tone, of approach. You can stand your ground, adult to adult, and ask the question again. This is the assertive route.

> 'What you just said didn't answer the question, in my opinion. So I'll ask it again . . .'

You can try assertiveness plus a dig:

> 'What you just said didn't answer the question. So I'll ask it again and hope this time you'll provide a more relevant/less hostile answer . . .'

You should be able to flip out of your initial role of uncomplicated interviewer into an assortment of others, all designed to assert your control of yourself and the interview. You could become a concerned comrade:

> 'It's not a good idea to get so riled. You'd best be careful or you might damage your health.'

You could try a put-down or two. Annoying a hostile interviewee can pay off because you win in two ways: they lose their temper and they lose control.

> 'So who's got their knickers in a twist now? And all I asked was . . .'

Or, if they're over about 45:

> 'Keep your hair on!'

If they're not someone you have to interview regularly and you can afford to annoy them, laugh at them. This will make you no friends but may provoke some good quotes. Power hates being mocked.

The monosyllabic

A nightmare, a challenge, the pits – the worst interviewees of all. They 'yes' or 'no' wherever they can, and answer 'can't say' or 'don't know' far too often. On the basis that they have agreed to be interviewed and so have something to gain from the exchange, the charitable approach is that they're tongue-tied, reticent, shy, upset, slow thinkers. They may well be any or all of those, though sometimes they're just bloody-minded, in a filthy temper, fed up or want to be rid of you.

The tactics in response are twofold. The first is to ease down, to talk more slowly and pause for at least four or five seconds before asking the next question. Really pause and look keen to learn the answer. Listen carefully without being too intense.

The second tactic is to ask precise questions that call for long, detailed answers. A flood victim, with three collapsed ceilings, replies 'Horrible' when asked 'What was it like?' Asked 'What did you do?' replies 'Panicked!' Asked 'What happened?', replies 'A pipe burst.'

The same flood victim, if asked 'Talk me through how you discovered the flood,' might reply:

> I'd been away for the weekend and came back to find water running down the hall. I went into the drawing room and water was dripping from the candelabra.
>
> I went upstairs to find the ceiling down and the room open to the loft, with the sky showing through. I had rockwool insulation in the loft and there was plaster and filthy rockwool everywhere, splattered up the walls, over the furniture. I panicked and ran round saying: 'Oh my God, oh my God.' Then I got a grip on myself and thought: 'You'd better turn the water off.' So I went down into the basement – which of course was flooded – and turned it off. After a while the dripping stopped and by that time something worse had occurred to me: had I paid my insurance?
>
> I dug out the policy and – mercifully – found that I had. There was a number to call and I called it. Within two hours three strong men had arrived and started heaving sodden carpets and rugs out and moving ruined sofas. They left a pump working in the basement and set up three dehumidifiers.

The questions to ask are the ones that call for descriptive answers:

> 'Tell me all about . . .'
>
> 'Talk me through exactly what happened . . .'
>
> 'Describe your day to me . . .'

Phrasing these questions takes practice, but it's worth all the effort in coaxing replies from this most challenging category of interviewees.

A last word from Lynn Barber, on interviewing bores: 'I found the only way was to ask completely batty questions, to try and startle them into saying something fresh.'

6
Quotes and checking your information

The interview is over. You're out of the door or you've put down the phone. If you've been recording the interview, your number one priority now is to listen back to ensure all is well. If you checked voice levels at the very beginning, and kept an eye on the recorder, there should be no problem, but accidents do happen.

Disasters

The editor of a famous women's magazine (who shall remain nameless) didn't discover that her recorder's batteries had failed after the first 10 minutes until she asked her secretary to type back her interview with Bob Geldof. If this should happen to you, you must do an immediate 'brain dump': write down every single thing you can remember about the interview. Don't panic – take several deep breaths and start by picturing yourself walking into the room to meet the interviewee, or being put through on the telephone. Closing your eyes often helps.

Write down your first impressions: what your interviewee was wearing, what the room looked like, the greeting. Go back to what you said and their response. Look again at your list of questions and try to hear the replies in your mind's ear. Write down everything. You'll be amazed how much you can remember, driven on by anxiety. Though you can phone back later to check on missing facts or spellings, remember that a repeat interview is never as successful, though it may be essential.

Journalists using shorthand are protected from the battery disaster. Their equivalent is the lost notebook, so always keep it close. If you're driving back from an interview, don't leave it in a briefcase in the car while you pay for petrol or have a cup of tea. Bags get snatched and cars get stolen.

For the same reason, if you're on a press trip abroad don't pack your notebook, photographs or any background material in luggage that goes in the hold, or leave them in a car or coach overnight.

Consider this horror story. After spending much of Friday interviewing a prickly interviewee and being lent some treasured drawings, the journalist is met from the train by her sister, throws her notebooks and the drawings into the back of the car, and off they go for a meal with friends. From there, they go out clubbing.

> We came out of the club at six in the morning. The car had been broken into. Everything had gone. Everything. My notes, the drawings, everything – and you know you can never recreate the freshness of an interview.
>
> We went home in total shock, went to bed and woke up to hear the phone ringing. Some woman in south London had found everything including my Filofax. She'd looked under M for mother and had rung her.
>
> We went round to the woman's house and found bits of paper hanging up to dry all over the place. The whole lot had been dumped in a puddle. I write in ink and the notes looked like watercolour drawings.
>
> I could see the odd word here and there, and luckily I can usually get it back if I transcribe my notes early enough. It was a nightmare. Thank goodness the drawings were in a plastic bag.

Interviewers with shorthand safely in the notebook, and those reassured that the recorder worked, can now make extra notes of everything significant that was said after the apparent 'end' of the interview, when the notebook was put away or the recorder turned off. These are often the most revealing comments of all; and, providing these notes are made immediately after an interview, they're also acceptable in court.

Shorthand interviewers who are going back to the office by train, bus, tube, car or taxi should grab the first opportunity to read back their notes, scribbling down any extra details. It's idiotic not to read back your notes the same day you do the interview. We've all made this mistake. Once.

If you can't read your notes, circle the offending words or sections and write down the letters/sounds you can read, leaving gaps to be filled.

Rather than racking your brains, leave the problem outlines for a while; you'll be surprised how easily the sense leaps out at you from the page when you read the notes a second time.

If you're playing back a recording with loads of background noise on it, play it over again and again, with the bass turned to its lowest setting and the treble to its highest.

Organisation

If a story is required immediately, it should be written directly from the notes. If the deadline is delayed, then it's best to type back your notes, though not necessarily in their entirety.

If you find gaps in the interview, facts or perhaps quotes you feel you should check with your interviewee, then go back to them as soon as possible. Provided you have 'left the door open' there should be no problem. If you haven't, you'll probably experience a mixture of exasperation (theirs) and embarrassment (yours).

Now is also the time to file away visiting cards and to update your contacts book, your email addresses, names, telephone numbers, postal addresses, even perhaps the names of your interviewee's partner/children/secretary.

What's missing?

After you've typed back your notes, read them again more analytically. What gaps are there? How best to fill them? What questions remain unanswered? Who might be able to help?

You must also consider how what you've learned might play in print. Is it libellous? Does anyone you've named need to be accorded the right to reply? Should you check with a third party to ensure that the story stands up?

If you haven't already done so, you should now compare what you've been told during the interview with what you discovered when researching. Are there any discrepancies? Do the statistics and the chronology agree? What follow-ups are needed? Think particularly hard about areas where your interviewee appeared reluctant to talk. Ask yourself, what is being covered up.

Checking

Never knowingly print anything false. Always strive to be accurate. This sounds moralistic, but it's the basis on which respect and reputations are built. Now, alas, it is applied more stringently and immediately to feature articles than to news, for which a 'post-now-correct-later' attitude is growing as a result of online demands.

In the United States, on the other hand, as Ian Katz of the *Guardian* discovered while on secondment to the Washington *Post*, the pressure can be not so much 'to get something into the paper than to get it exactly right'. He recounts how his first piece for the *Post*'s Style section finally appeared two weeks after he thought he had finished it, after daily discussions with an editor who wanted hazy details checked and extra quotes sought, and who made detailed structural and stylistic requests.

> I would like to round off the story by reporting that the finished product was not markedly better than my first offering, that it had been robbed of some of its immediacy, even. What a ringing endorsement that would be for the British way of doing things. But it was better, immeasurably so. And in the two (pretty miserable) weeks of editing, I probably learnt more than I had in a year of British journalism.

He has just one qualifier, relating to the *Post*'s virtual monopoly. 'It is hard to imagine editors being quite as fastidious if four broadsheet competitors were dropping on the back bench every night.'

Never misreport or, if there are gaps in your notes, guess – or your editor might soon be the recipient of a letter as damaging and astringent as this from Jeremy Paxman to the editor of the *Financial Times*.

> Sir . . .
>
> It is a pity your correspondent [the writer responsible for 'Of monsters and lesser mortals', a report of a meal with the journalist and author Robert Harris] cannot tell the difference between a Gothic Victorian vicarage standing in under one acre of garden and an 18th century pile 'sitting on huge swathes of land in Berkshire' . . .
>
> Your correspondent alleges Robert rolled a Cuban cigar 'between his manicured fingers'. Robert is certainly a stranger to the thrills of DIY. But if his hands have ever been buffed and polished by a manicurist, I will personally service his Jaguar.

> Your correspondent finally goes on to relate how he 'spluttered' into his '£15 goblet of brandy' at the size of the bill. I really cannot fathom his discomfort, since, when given the choice by Robert of whether they would eat at the local pub or Albert Speer's expensive eatery, your correspondent opted for the latter, with the words: 'The FT will pay'.

For a daily reminder of the pits into which careless interviewers may fall, the *Guardian*'s corrections and clarifications column is unsurpassed.

Sight of copy?

Showing interviewees their copy before it's published is something many journalists say they don't do, won't do. They regard it as wimpish, an admission of inadequacy. But some journalists check the copy – because it's part of the agreement, because they want to avoid trouble, or – with a complex, technical subject because they wish to ensure the facts are right.

Freelance Janet Barber remembers a profile she did for *She* magazine of the then youngest local government chief executive in the country. 'He was 30 and completely stiff. He had a suit and spectacles and was completely respectable. I battled along with the interview but could not get the show on the road.' She did the best feature she could, working with what she had.

The magazine sent the copy out for checking, as it always did then, and the chief executive phoned her. 'He said: "I realise this has got absolutely no personality about it. It's my fault. I'm new to this sort of thing. Would it be helpful if you could come back and talk to me again? So I went back, had lunch with him, his wife and two of his children.'

This time she got a much more lively interview with more vivid details – such as what was his usual breakfast: 'A Mars bar and a can of Coke.'

Editing quotes

Quotes are used to add life, to brighten copy, to emphasise a point, to move the story along, but *not* because you want to fill space or show the world you can use a recorder.

How much do you change what interviewees say? As little as possible. Do you quote them accurately? Of course. Just as they know how to spell their own names, they know what words they use.

A journalist on a teen magazine asked a fashion PR for quotes on cut-price shopping. He remembers it clearly. 'She came round to interview me at home with a photographer, who took pix around my flat. It was informal. We chatted and I told them all sorts of things which they obviously didn't write down in detail, because when the interview came out I was horrified.' He still has the offending cutting and quotes from it.

> *One looks so seedy* . . . I never use the word *one*. I despise it. They got the gist but didn't get the details right.
>
> Here, about shoes, it says *When they're scuffed or holey or worn down one looks so seedy and it's not so easy to get away with wearing second-hand clothes.* I am sure I said something along those lines because it makes sense, but it's not my language. What they printed is like girl talk.
>
> Here, it says *I never use soap.* Not true. *My skin's dry.* It's not. *It's vital to moisturise my skin.* I would have used more blokey talk.

Contrary to received wisdom, most interviewees talk coherently. This is particularly true if the interviewer focuses her mind and asks precise questions. Disorganised people and very fast thinkers may give answers which jump about all over the place, but in these days of media training there aren't so many of them.

With most interviewees, then, the best guideline is tidy up, snip out 'ums' and 'ers', but never, ever, change the sense. You can patch – take something they said at one point and link it with another sentence they used earlier – as long as you use their words and keep the meaning secure.

What if they said something vivid and quotable but not in a nice, neat, tidy sentence? There's no law that insists quotes must have subject, verb and object.

> 'As cuddly as a cut-throat razor,' was how Sir Peter Parker described . . .

This has plenty of impact, probably more so by being a snippet.

It's important to quote accurately, but do you quote *exactly* what people say? Let's start with swearing. If a pop star's every second word is 'fuck' or 'shit', do you print it?

In a laddish mag, probably yes. Though the frequency of swear words might be reduced, you try to give a realistic impression of how the star talks. If the interview is for a middle-ground family publication, then it's the editor's decision whether to use 'f***' and 's**t'. If the interview is for a sub-teen magazine, then probably not at all. It's possible to cut the swearing and still keep the quotes.

The choice is to print accurately, cut, or suggest. What is not acceptable is substituting a totally different word. You don't use 'excrement' in place of 'shit' or 'sex' instead of 'fuck'.

What about correcting grammar? If an interviewee says 'Less than a thousand people turned up', would you change that to 'Fewer than a thousand people turned up'? For most newspapers, you would, because that's what they do.

We are now entering writers-versus-subs territory. I'd like to suggest (NB 'suggest') that on free-thinking publications you might not change the quote, unless the interviewee had said during the interview that they'd like their quotes tidied up or changed so that they read grammatically. I believe we're here to print what the interviewee said, not what the chief sub wished they'd said. But be warned: this is heresy. Quite a few tutors strongly disagree.

If the interviewee says 'Not one of the nine reasons are valid', do you change that to 'Not one of the nine reasons is valid'? Again, I'd say no. If you work on a writer's paper, this just might be acceptable. If you work on a sub's paper, it may well be changed. You will know it's not what they said, your interviewee will know it's not what they said, but English grammar will have triumphed. Here endeth the heresy.

However, since the prime reason for writing is to communicate, something has to be done if the interviewee uses obscure words.

> 'What sort of writer is the English professor looking for?'
> 'He wants a sesquipedalian, of course.'

Interesting but mystifying. You've got to explain what 'sesquipedalian' is and fairly quickly.

> 'I live in a duplex.'

Duplex?

This is why square brackets were invented.

> 'He wants a sesquipedalian, of course [someone who loves and tends to use long words].'
>
> 'I live in a duplex [a maisonette].'

So no changing quotes, please, just clarifying them. 'You can presume intelligence but not knowledge' – one of the great journalistic principles.

If you reckon your interviewee knows what they are talking about, then – however weird the quote may be – either check it or leave it as is. Years ago, I interviewed the famous American newspaperman Scott Newhall, about a feud with a rival Californian editor who'd accused him in print of being a 'liberal' – an insupportable insult. Scott had challenged the other editor to meet him under the Federal Savings and Loan clock at noon and defied him to 'repeat the slander'.

Back in Britain, I wavered and havered. Obviously he meant 'libel', not 'slander'. Should I change it or not? I couldn't reach Newhall and the deadline loomed, so eventually I decided he must have said it deliberately and used his words.

The story was picked up by *Press Gazette* and the writer made the point – which had completely missed me – that using the word 'slander' was an insult. The rival paper was so insignificant that no one read it, ergo the slur had to be slander.

Ridicule

Should you ridicule people by quoting exactly what they say? Only if you want to make a fool of them. If you interview someone you heartily dislike, a vainglorious prat who spends half the interview boasting about their love for classical music and then talks about 'Beethoven's Erotica Symphony', do you change that to 'Beethoven's Eroica Symphony'? Only you can decide. What you *don't* do, in my opinion, is write 'Beethoven's Erotica Symphony (sic)'. If you do, you're the pompous prat then.

If they are incoherent and you don't wish to make a fool of them, your course is simple: turn what they say into reported speech. Don't succumb to the tyranny of the recorder.

Supposedly, the higher the position the person occupies whether by election or selection, the more they become used to criticism. Supposedly. It's a sad truth that very few of us can accurately judge what respect a person believes they deserve.

The capacity to be insulted is said to be directly and inversely related to intelligence. But the capacity to be offended by contested quotes in print is limitless. And if what you print is true, that just makes them more furious – with you.

'Sourcing'

When it comes to writing up a suspect statement or fact, 'source it' is the safest advice, that is, attribute it to the speaker and/or put what's said inside quote marks. Depending on what you've been told, you might run it past the lawyers.

'There's no truth in the rumour that we're separating' is safer than the same words turned into reported speech. 'The marketing manager said, "Sales are 60% up since March"' is wiser than reporting that 'the company's sales have risen 60% over the last six months', though 'The marketing manager reports that the company's sales have risen 60% over the last six months' will do.

Last word

Finally, what do you do when your interviewee 'doesn't trouble the note-taker' – in other words, when your interviewee absolutely refuses to talk. Answer: you make the best of a bad job. Occasionally it's possible to turn rejection into rejoicing. Here's a rare and treasured example.

A London paper commissioned film columnist William Hall to find and interview the elusive Marlon Brando, who'd just finished *Last Tango in Paris* and was about to win an Oscar for *The Godfather*. Hall tracked him down to his hideaway in Tahiti and, after three weeks of cat-and-mouse chase, cornered him one morning at 5.45 am.

> I still remember this 22 stone of raging bull bursting out of his bedroom to confront me on the back terrace as the dawn came up. He was wearing only a colourful sarong around his ample waist.

Brando was furious and refused to talk. Did Hall despair? Of course not. He wrote a famous feature recounting how he discovered Marlon Brando's South Sea Island bolt hole. The entire 'interview' consisted of just two sentences.

> 'I'm going to give you to the count of three and then I'm going to punch you right in the face,' was Brando's welcome. His lips were white and his eyes were glazed. He waved hairy knuckles under my nose and bellowed: 'I'm warning you, there's going to be great physical personal damage done to you.'

Hall was then chased around the fish pond, through the house and onto the porch, before Brando waved a fist in final farewell, slamming the door and, as Hall recounts, giving him 'the best story of his entire career'.

Hall also claims the shortest interview ever, with Vivien Leigh, when she was filming on the Hollywood set of *Ship of Fools*. 'I had no idea she was close to a breakdown when the director introduced us and then walked away,' he says. 'I was left holding this limp hand, gazing into a pair of mad eyes.'

'What an honour, Miss Leigh,' he said. 'And when are we going to have the pleasure of welcoming you back to London?'

'God knows,' she answered and walked off.

Being the journalist he is, Hall got a diary lead out of that.

7
Note-taking and recording

Journalists make notes so they can write accurate stories containing the required mix of facts, colour, background, anecdotes and quotes. They aim to avoid those dread words: 'There's been a complaint . . .'

To make notes they use shorthand, longhand scribble, recorder or memory. Which they opt for is a trade-off between what they want from the interview, the skills they possess, the time available and the sensitivity or temperament of the interviewee. For interviewees they know well, journalists can walk in carrying an open notebook. With the elusive or reclusive, they may decide not to bring out a recorder until they judge their interviewee has relaxed. There are obviously no concerns like these when phoning.

Some write reams during the interview, some write nothing. Some write surreptitiously on notebooks under the table or even in their jacket pockets – though how readable jacket-pocket notes are is debatable. There are investigative reporters who are 'wired' for sound and vision.

Each approach has its strengths and drawbacks, but there are two enduring principles. First, few journalists regret learning shorthand. What they regret is letting it rust. Second, however good you think your memory is, it's fallible, so don't overstretch it.

There's no one best method. It all depends what you're after. If it's a 1,000-word profile of a rising celebrity, requiring good quotes and plenty of description to be delivered within a week, then recorder and notebook used in tandem will probably work best. If what's wanted is a 200-word news story, deadline in an hour, then use the phone and shorthand. For a face-to-face anecdote from a nervous friend about a freshly convicted criminal? Memory, with story committed to notebook asap (really asap).

Electronic

Digital recorders are popular with journalists because of the protection they afford. They're now available on phones, laptops, computers, cameras and who knows what else by the time this book is published.

They are great for face-to-face profiles, allowing the interviewer to concentrate totally on the interviewee. Mini 'snoop/spy' video cameras, which film from inside sports bags etc., now form part of many investigative reporters' equipment.

For:

- Provide proof of what was said. 'To err is human, to get it on tape divine' is said to be the motto of *News of the World* investigative reporters.
- You get the feeling of truth into your quotes.
- Enable you to concentrate on your interviewee and, face-to-face, establish excellent eye contact.
- Most interviewees soon forget they're being taped and talk freely.
- If the interviewee is a fast talker, you don't have to slow them down to get quotes. Digital recorders are particularly useful with phone interviews. Editors trust them.
- Interviewees who know they have been recorded rarely question the accuracy of quotes.
- You can interview in a car or other moving vehicle where writing may be difficult.

Against:

- Without using a notebook at the same time, you can't record gestures, the colour of the interviewee's eyes, the state of their desk or the ambience.
- Not suitable for large group interviews.
- Batteries can go flat.
- Some don't work particularly well in noisy places such as restaurants or factories.
- Can take hours to transcribe.
- You may have to listen many times.
- Face-to-face, seem to encourage over-quoting, often of banal words.

Some negative aspects can easily be countered: ensuring the batteries are fresh, for instance. If you have a recorder with a counter and cue marker, it shouldn't be necessary to listen back several times. Just listen once and mark the best quotes, then you can go straight to them later.

The reluctant interviewee is more difficult. In business journalism it's usually only villains who object to being recorded, but elsewhere there are some inexperienced, nervous, often older interviewees who genuinely experience mike fright. Time for persuasion and sweet talk.

For a portable recorder, best go for one with a counter, indicator light and an adjustable as well as omni-directional mike. This is particularly helpful in noisy restaurants or crowded rooms.

If you have a voice-activated recording facility on your recorder, ensure it's permanently taped off, and if for face-to-face interviews you carry your recorder in a packed bag, make certain the play/record facility is locked off, too, or you could arrive with flat batteries.

Written

Interviewees do not want to be misquoted, so are reassured to see a notebook. There's no need to apologise when you produce one: it's the journalist's calling card. But produce it at the right time, use it properly and don't lose it. Pens or ballpoints with permanent ink are advisable.

Daft as it may sound to beginners, there really is one best way of using a spiral bound 'reporter's' notebook and that is to go right the way through on one side of the paper to the end and, providing it's good-quality paper, then turn the book over and come back. Once you've started writing, then turning the *book* rather than the paper is a recipe for disaster.

Every interview must be dated, and it's not a bad idea to make a contents list on the inside front and inside back covers. This helps to locate interviews should you need to refer to them again. Don't rip pages out of your notebook. It's a bad habit to get into and could destroy proof of what an interviewee had said and give the appearance of tampering with evidence, which could be dangerous should there be a legal query or complaint.

What size notebook? For face-to-face, some people think A4 is too big, too floppy, intimidating and hard to use. Bound or spiral-bound A5 notebooks suit many but seem to be losing some ground to smaller A6 books, which can be put in a jacket pocket or handbag. In America there is a specially sized Pitman shorthand notebook, 10.1 cm × 20.3 cm, ruled with faint interlines. For telephone interviews, when you don't need to keep your notes shielded, an A4 notebook on your desk works well.

Advice for beginners: don't put the questions down in your notebook leaving space underneath for the answers. Answers are never the length estimated and doing this ties you into a sequence, inhibiting those all-important follow-up questions. Always have your questions separate. It's not a bad idea to devise some sort of code you can use for an instant edit while you make notes. Two lines by the side of a good quote, for instance; a cross to show you need to go back again for more information.

Because so much is going on during an interview – listening to answers, checking for consistency, appraising, planning future questions and making notes as well – it's worth considering keeping a running note of what has to be checked when an opportunity arises, without interrupting or spoiling the flow.

At the top of the page, write the key points still to be checked as they occur to you. As you turn the page, if you haven't managed to have your queries answered, carry them over until the opportunity arises. The alternative is to mark clearly in the margin points you think you'll need to return to later; then, towards the end of the interview, scan your notes to check what remains to be clarified.

Longhand scribble

For:

- Simple.
- OK with a very, very slow speaker, perhaps; or where you're interviewing in a foreign language and everything is translated from English into another language and then back again.
- Just about suitable for statistics, short facts.

Against:

- Slow. Causes hold-ups for catch-ups. Particularly annoying for phone interviews.
- Unimpressive.
- Relies heavily on memory.

- Not good for lively quotes.
- Advice: only if you must – much better to learn Teeline.

Shorthand

For:

- Minimal, inexpensive equipment.
- Works almost everywhere, unhampered by noise, magnets, being dropped etc.
- Immediately accessible, that is, no need to rewind and listen back.
- Acceptable in law if notes are taken during the interview or almost immediately after the interview closed.
- Some interviewees are impressed, ditto colleagues; looks good on CVs.
- About four to five times faster than longhand.

Against:

- Takes time to learn.
- Minimises eye contact.
- Looks old-fashioned to some interviewees, particularly celebrities.
- Unless note-taker is very skilled, should be read back quickly.
- Unlike tapes, not verbatim.
- Chance of errors in both note-taking and transcription.

The main shorthand systems taught in the English-speaking world are, in order of invention, Gregg, Pitman's New Era, Speedwriting, Teeline and Pitman 2000. Generally speaking, the easier a system is to learn, the longer it will take to write. What makes a system easy to learn is simple theory and a light memory load (not too many short forms). What holds you up is complicated theory, when you have to stop and think: 'Is that written up or down, with a loop or a hook?'

However, it's reading it back that counts, and systems in which the theory is simple and the vowels are included in what's written down are generally easy to read back. The more the system depends on placement on or above the line, on thick or thin strokes and on short forms, then the harder it is to read back.

The system favoured by most British journalists is Teeline, invented in 1967 by journalist James Hill who was unhappy with existing choices. The memory load is light and the theory can be learnt in 20 hours.

Teeline students regularly reach 100 wpm within a term, doing shorthand just six or seven hours a week for 12 weeks. Some trainees on the PMA Training nine-week postgraduate journalism course reach 100 wpm in just under 30 hours. Top achievable speeds with Teeline are 130–140 wpm, quite enough for most working journos.

This is a system vaunted for its accuracy and taught by the BBC and on the National Council for the Training of Journalists (NCTJ) courses. Students attaining 100 per cent accuracy with Teeline are said to outnumber other systems' students by four to one. Its critics say it's too flexible, allowing people to develop their own version. Others think this a plus. A book highly recommended by experienced tutors is *Teeline Fast* by Ann Dix. Nothing is said to come anywhere near it.

Pitman 2000 has a ceiling speed of 120–130 wpm and a middling-heavy memory load (83 short forms). However, it has all the problems of a system based on the fountain pen, where thick and thin strokes and placement on, above or below the line are critical. If you're using a ballpoint pen on unlined paper, one shape could be read as 'see' or 'easy' 'ass' or 'essay', and because Pitman's is a phonetic rather than alphabetic system, it can be a handicap when interviewing in a foreign language – as I discovered when I interviewed a Japanese cognac blender who spoke in French. There was the added complication of the Japanese inability to pronounce the letter L. Experiences like these teach you to take a recorder as well.

For journalists who need shorthand of 130 wpm and above, there are two choices: Pitman New Era with ceiling speeds of 250 wpm, and Gregg Simplified, ceiling speed 200 wpm. Pitman New Era, launched in 1922, has fairly complex theory, a very heavy memory load of 400 short forms, and relies on placement, thick and thin strokes and omitting vowels at speed.

Parliamentary reporters working for Hansard take notes for about 10 minutes at a stretch, some using Pitman's New Era, others stenographic machines, yet others transcribing from tapes. Of those who use shorthand, around 80 per cent have such a precise 'note' it can be read back by others.

Sadly, Gregg Simplified, though widespread in the United States, has to be ruled out in Britain except by the determined who can track down the few enthusiastic and dedicated Gregg teachers, who like its integral vowels and the fact that once a rule is learnt it is never modified. It would have taken hold in Britain but for the Americans. Dr John Gregg, the Irishman who developed it, went off to the United States in 1893 when he discovered someone was going to bring out his system in Chicago under another name. He never returned.

Speedwriting has an 80–100 wpm ceiling. It's easy to learn but takes huge effort to get up to any speed so is not suitable for most journalists.

You should use shorthand for facts, comments and really good quotes – not for every word. That just causes extra work reading back, weary wrists and overfull notebooks. An expense of spirit in wasteful action.

It takes time and practice with shorthand not to take down too much. You have to learn to edit as you go along. This comes from knowing your brief, and understanding what interests the reader. Reports and features crammed with too many quotes are often indigestible.

Whether you're left-handed or right-handed makes no difference to the ability to write shorthand. What does make a difference is IQ and mind-set. Shorthand expert Harry Butler has said that the analytical can have problems.

If you want to know your shorthand potential, here's a do-it-yourself aptitude test. Type a few paragraphs (at least 50 words) and print them out in at least double spacing. Then ask a friend to time you or time yourself and see how many words you can write under the printed words in the space of a minute.

- If you've written 40–50 words, your speed potential is 120 wpm.
- If you've written about 35 words, your potential is 100 wpm.
- If you've written about 25 words, your potential is 80 wpm.

A final thought about shorthand. At an aviation press conference a journalist from *Travel Trade Gazette* found that her pen had run out.

> I went through my bag and realised I hadn't a spare. I'd left the office in a hurry and there was nobody there I knew to borrow from. I rooted around and found my eyeliner. I used it as the lightest possible shorthand.

And yes, they used the story. You couldn't have done that with longhand.

Slow, slow, quick, quick, slow

There are bound to be times when your note-taking lags. How you buy time is your choice. Some journalists advise throwing in a soft 'filler' question and just not listening to the answer while catching up. Easier said than done. Others repeat back with admiration or amazement the answer or quote they are busy writing down. Yet again, others say: 'Sorry, you're going a little fast. Would you hold on a second, please?'

Reading back

The rule is to read back your notes as soon as possible, certainly within a few hours, while your memory of the interview is still fresh. You'll be glad you did. Short-term memory fades quickly and another, intervening interview can drive recollection of strange words or speech patterns clean out of your head. So don't let the sun go down on your unread notebook.

Memory

For:

- Face-to-face puts nervous, apprehensive interviewees at ease (but worries experienced interviewees who will wonder how good your memory is).
- Relaxed, chatty interviewees often give better quotes.

Against:

- Memory is notoriously and demonstrably unreliable.
- Unless notes are made immediately after the interview with the time recorded, they are vulnerable to attack in a court of law (see also opposite).

Actors and counsellors, who have been trained to remember, do well at recalling conversations; most journalists less so. Reporters' confidence in their memory over a protracted interview is usually misplaced. That doesn't mean you should always have your notebook in your hand. When you first meet someone, before the interview proper has begun, your interviewee may say something eminently quotable. Remember it and write it down as soon as you get your notebook out.

Again, at the end of the interview, when you've put your notebook away and are just chatting, your interviewee may let slip some valuable information. Don't hoick your notebook out, but take the first opportunity after leaving to write it down. Note the time, too.

Notes made during and immediately after an interview are acceptable in court. Memory is much more likely to be probed and put to the test. Police notes are accepted as evidence, so there's no reason for journalists to be defensive about relying on their shorthand.

It's a rare journalist who boasts about their shorthand. They may have reached 100 smoothly dictated words a minute during training and be rightly proud – but they soon realise that 100 wpm is not the answer when interviewing, because almost all interviewees talk at well over 100 wpm and lots of them will use long words.

This means that those who don't solve the problem by using recorders have to develop a technique that will enable them to select and accurately note what they judge the important sections of what they hear. Generally they do this by writing down as fast as they can key words and sentences, using a scribbled mixture of shorthand and longhand.

It's for this reason that rather messy notebooks are rarely on show, but there is one to be found in the Hutton Inquiry report (an inquiry set up to examine circumstances surrounding the death of Dr Kelly in 2003, the year Iraq was invaded).

Susan Watts (BBC's Newsnight's science editor) had interviewed Kelly and was called to give evidence. Her interview notes are well worth a look, including *Teeline*, doodles and scribbles.

Available at:

www.the-hutton-inquiry.org.uk/content/evidence-lists/evidence-sjw.htm and www.the-hutton-inquiry.org.uk/content/sjw/sjw_1_0025to0029.pdf.

8
Interviewing for the internet

Brendan Martin

The face of journalism has changed greatly since the previous edition of this book. The internet has taken hold of mass communication in a way few would have imagined a decade ago. Journalists now write and report news and features in a variety of formats.

With the ever-rising cost of newsprint, not to mention the need to preserve the Earth's resources, many publishers are turning to online publishing as a way of extending their print brand. Some have ceased to publish print editions and are on the web only. An increasing number of titles are appearing in both print and online formats. For you the interviewer, online publishing brings new challenges as greater demands are put upon you. But these challenges can raise the quality of your journalism.

Although the mainstay of any interviewer is a notebook and pen, the technology has developed at a great pace. Few people today use tape recorders. Apart from anything else, have you ever tried to buy a cassette recorder lately? They are hard to find.

The dictaphone has given way to the digital recorder, while even the iconic iPod can double as a recording device. But sound recording itself is fast becoming an ancient art. The advent of the handheld digital video recorder now allows you to record your interview in both sound and vision. Many journalists find that a few hundred pounds spent on a video camera is a good investment.

Others, such as Dan Ilett, editor and owner of the environmental business news service Greenbang (www.greenbang.com), says he does not even bother with a video camera. 'I use my phone and find I get acceptable results. I can record up to 15 minutes on that. The newer phones have larger memory and can record for longer.'

Questions have to be more direct. Treat it like a live interview.

Planning your questions

In the same way that planning forms an integral part of an interview just for print, good preparation is essential for something you want to use online. The difference is in how you phrase your questions.

The longer you make your video or audio clip, the less your audience will like it. The nature of the internet is brevity, speed and instant communication. You would be far better uploading a single 15-second soundbite within minutes of your interviewee saying it than waiting hours or even days to edit, polish and upload a five-minute package.

The beauty of the web is that you can do both. Upload your soundbite as soon as you can and use it to trail the fuller interview that you will put online later.

The questions you put to your interviewee need to be short and sharp. As you are looking to produce short interviews, you need to get to the point quite quickly.

> 'This new CD you have produced traces your musical youth in Liverpool and is influenced by many of the people you knew at the time. How did that come about?'
>
> 'What made you produce a CD tracing your musical youth in Liverpool and the people you knew at the time?'

Both these questions are open and allow the interviewee to speak. The second one is shorter and therefore better for your online interview.

Another consideration when asking a question is that, as you edit it for upload, you need to let your audience know what you are talking about.

> 'What is the new one about?'

This doesn't tell us what you're talking about.

> 'What is your new book about?'

This does.

Conducting your interview

As with all interviews, your online interview is just a controlled conversation between two people in which one tries to elicit information from the other. If the task is the same, so are the ground rules. You need to establish rapport; you need to tell the interviewee the general areas you wish to cover; and you need to listen.

'But I'm filming it,' I hear you cry. 'I can listen to it when I play it back.' You can indeed, but you cannot ask follow-up questions. Trust me, you have to listen.

Some of the tricks of the trade of print interviewing apply to online interviews. Remember to use silence as a method of getting your interviewee to talk. Don't worry about the gap in the conversation, you can always edit it out.

The 'sandwich technique' is also very useful. Ask a nice question first, then sandwich a nasty second question between the first and the third, which is also a nice question.

Video recording the interview

When you meet your interviewee and exchange greetings, let them know you're going to record the interview for possible use on the internet. If you are using a video camera or a camera phone, it allows them to make sure they are happy with the way they look. An interviewee who is self-conscious about their appearance is an interviewee who will not give of their best.

If you are conducting the interview alone, try to have your video camera on a tripod. There are small ones available at good photographic shops as well as chain stores. This will avoid camera shake and the inevitable amateur look.

If you have to hold the camera by hand, make sure you hold it to one side of you. Do not let it block your eye-to-eye contact with your interviewee. It is more usual to take someone with you to do the filming while you concentrate on the interviewing.

You must also check that you can hear the interviewee. If you have a digital video camera with a microphone port, you would be well advised to buy an external microphone that you can hold or clip onto the interviewee's clothing. Some background noise is good, but not too much.

Ilett adds some practical legal advice: 'If there is background music playing in the background, try to avoid recording it. If you replay this interview as a podcast, you might be asked to pay for the rights to broadcast the music!'

Unless you have invested in some professional lighting, make sure you film in a well-lit area. 'You would be surprised how many people forget to have the light or the sun behind them. Never shoot into the light source or even have it shining into the camera from a sideways position,' says Ilett.

When interviewing for film, pause in between each question and answer. This allows you to edit the recording more easily afterwards. Keep your mobile phone switched off (unless you're filming with it).

Audio recording the interview

This is easier because you don't have to worry about the pictures. And the interviewee doesn't worry about their looks. Again, make sure you are picking up the sound properly.

An interview recorded just for your reference can have background noise and changing sound. You are just using this type of recording simply to recall what was said so that you can write it up. But an audio interview to be broadcast on the internet must be of high standard.

After the interview

Editing the interview for uploading to the internet can be a relatively easy task. There are many audio editing software programs available, Quicktime and Apple's iMovie being just two excellent ones. But there are lots of others around, with more being developed all the time. Some are free and can be downloaded from the internet.

Once you have mastered the technicalities of the sound editing software, you need to make editorial decisions about what to use and what to discard. This is exactly the same sort of decision you make when selecting material for print.

However, more than ever you are looking for 'bell-ringers' – sentences or phrases that leap out at you from the recording as great quotes.

When working at *TVTimes* I interviewed Paul McCartney about his life and times. At one point I asked him if there was anything left in life he still wanted to achieve. His answer rang like Big Ben in my head.

> 'Is there any ambition left that you want to fulfil?' I asked him.
>
> 'Uhm', he replied. 'I've got writing which I do all the time when I have a day off. And I've got this vague idea that I'm going to get a band together and go back on the road. Obviously, I can't play to many more people than I have already. And I can't get much higher in the charts than No 1. So I think all my ambitions have been achieved. So it's hard when people say "Paul, what can you do next? What can you do to top what you've possibly done?" I've thought about that and I'm still trying to write a really great song. You know, I've written . . .'

Whoa! What was that he said?

> 'I'm still trying to write a really great song.'

This is the man who wrote *Yesterday*, *Let it be*, *Eleanor Rigby*, *Hey Jude* and *Penny Lane*, among others.

Naturally, the subs took that quote from my interview and featured it as a pull quote on the final page layout.

Using that surprising admission from one of the twentieth century's greatest songwriters as a soundbite on a website would not have been easy. McCartney's response to my question started with an 'Uhm' and was followed by several predictable sentences, then he said: 'I'm still trying to write a really great song.'

To have tried to clean up that recording and edit it would have been time-consuming. Not difficult, but listeners would have heard the leap in the background sound where material was cut out.

You can't fake a closed answer

In print, you can always 'fake' a closed answer. No, I don't mean you make it up! If you ask a closed question:

'Is it your belief that this government is not doing enough to help the elderly?'
'Yes.'

In print, you could write:

The Leader of the Opposition said he believed that this government is not doing enough to help the elderly.

Online, all you could show your audience is a politician answering:

'Is it your belief that this government is not doing enough to help the elderly?'
'Yes.'

Not terribly impressive is it?

Open questions, as has been explained elsewhere, are the easiest and most used way to getting information. Closed questions are used to confirm or deny. When used in that manner, they can be more powerful on the internet.

'Are you planning to cut back jobs in your three factories?'
'No.'

That would appear on the page thus:

'The CEO denied that there will be job cuts at his company's three factories.'

On the internet, the CEO looks heartless and uncaring if he gives a monosyllabic answer to such an important question. More so, if you allow the clip to run on to show he said nothing else.

Rules were made to be broken

Well, if not broken, then bent a little. Many editors don't like interviews that are just 'Question and Answer' sessions (Q&As as they're called). When I commission a writer to interview someone, if they come back with a Q&A they are left in no doubt as to my views. I, and many other editors, consider the Q&A to be lazy journalism. Anyone can transcribe a recording, put the questions into italics, and save the file.

The art of the good Q&A is to convert the recording into a proper interview that captures the colour, the essence of the interviewee, and all their nuances. Then write it in a Q&A format.

The inside back page of *Radio Times* (titled 'One Final Question') has examples of this every week. The skill of the interviewers who write this page can be seen from the way they drop a light question into the piece every so often. It allows the personality of the interviewee to shine.

On the internet the Q&A is one of the best ways of presenting an interview in a text format. Research has shown – and continues to show – that users of the internet read only about 25% of the amount they would when presented with the same information in traditional hard copy. They scan.

The eye seeks out the material the brain is interested in reading. To aid with this scanning process, writing on the web is shorter and sharper. It is presented in smaller chunks. Paragraphs have spaces between them whereas magazine and newspaper text does not.

Bullet points and lists are important tools in the armoury of the internet journalist and web designer. So with the Q&A.

Online text Q&A

The internet's style is modern, friendly and less formal than much traditional print media. Consequently, the online Q&A interview can be like this too. For a text interview that reflects this informality but yet extracts information from the interviewee, go online and take a look at this link: www.time.com/time/arts/article/0,8599,1687229,00.html (interview with Stephen King in *Time* magazine, November 2007).

New methods of interviewing

Instant messaging (IM)

This is a very popular method of conversing on the internet. It can also be used for interviews. IM works as a simple typed conversation. The advantages are that the interviewer types in their question and the interviewee replies with a live answer. You can then ask a follow-up question. It's instant – hence the name.

IM is very good for interviewing people who don't want other people in the office to see them talking. They simply type innocently on their keyboard and no one knows they are having a conversation.

The disadvantages are that there is no human contact. You don't see your interviewee. Indeed, you have no actual proof that you are talking to the person you think you are. Film stars and politicians have been known to have a PR or other employee conduct the interview for them.

Email

Another method is email – if that is the only way to get to an interviewee. In reality, this method is pretty unsatisfactory for an interview of any length or depth. The email interview should only be used to check or confirm facts. But again, beware, you can never be sure the response has come from the person you've interviewed. Usually these are intercepted by some scheming PR. Furthermore, they can take some time to reply.

Outlets for your interviews

Blogs

A blog, short for 'weblog', is an online diary or journal. Blogs started as a way for individuals to publish their thoughts, anecdotes and other bits of writing on the web. Now many publishers are using blogs as part of the content they offer.

Radio Times (www.radiotimes.com) offers blogs by many of its columnists. This gives the audience new material by writers they enjoy and the opportunity to take part in debate. BBC Radio 4's afternoon current affairs programme *PM* (www.bbc.co.uk/radio4/news/pm) also offers listeners a chance to interact with the show.

A blog can contain text, images and audio and video files – just the sort of place you can post the full version of an interview that may have appeared in a truncated form in print.

Podcasts

A podcast is defined as 'A series of digital-media files which are distributed over the internet using syndication feeds for playback on portable media players and computers.' (Wikipedia).

In reality it's just like a short radio programme made into a format that can be downloaded to an MP3 or MP4 player or a computer. If you are a freelance journalist who wants to get your work to a wide audience, podcasting is a way to do this.

You can use a podcatcher, which is nothing more than a piece of software that distributes your podcast around the internet. A freelance would probably find it more productive and certainly less costly to use an established podcaster such as Apple iTunes. (A podcaster is the online equivalent of a broadcaster.) This dominant podcaster gets your work to a wide audience. By keeping check on the internet and the changes that happen almost daily, you will be able to find other podcasters should you need them.

If you are on the staff of, or contributing to, an established publication, they will usually podcast your material for you. It will, as you would expect, be done under their brand name.

The BBC makes available podcasts of many of its programmes (www.bbc.co.uk/radio/podcasts/directory/). Many are selections from longer shows edited into compilation packages; others feature sections of major news programmes such as *Today* and *PM*. Listen to some of these to hear how they edit an interview into a podcast.

Your perceptive and probing print interview reaches the public when the magazine or newspaper is distributed to the shops or pushed through your readers' letterboxes. The equivalent interview for online broadcast, that is, your podcast, is made available to your audience by the use of podcasting hosts. (They're a sort of online equivalent of a wholesale distributor and newsagent's shop rolled into one.)

You can deliver your podcast yourself but it's unlikely you'll have the resources as a one-person band to do that. This is why there are websites that host podcasts.

There are several good podcasting hosts: Apple's iTunes is the best known. Others to look at include jellycast (www.jellycast.com) and Tubemogul (www.tubemogul.com). The latter publishes all your video podcasts – or vodcasts (a vodcast is the same as a podcast but with the added ingredient of video) – on about 10 different websites called 'hosting platforms'. Well, there is no point in doing your interview if you cannot get it out to a potential audience.

Internet radio (streaming)

At the time of writing, there are several hundred radio stations broadcasting live exclusively on the internet. Many are professional stations run by the BBC and others. Some are amateur outfits, but many of these provide a very professional service. Interviews frequently form a part of the mix such stations offer.

These interviews are similar to those broadcast on conventional radio and should be conducted in the same manner. If there is a difference it is the need to remember you have a worldwide audience, and consequently terms, locations, times and colloquialisms need explanation – though not at the expense of the interview. Try to form your questions in a manner that the majority of the listeners will understand. But perhaps the most important point to remember about interviewing for the internet is summed up in the conclusion below.

Conclusion

With so many new methods of gathering and conveying information, it would be easy to think the basic skills of interviewing have changed. They have not. An interview remains a dialogue in which one person listens and the other talks.

9 Interviewing politicians

As interviewees, politicians are a breed apart. Even experienced journalists rate them as difficult, and for good reason: most politicians are wary, guileful and well trained. My first interview with an MP ended with him slowly and distinctly dictating his thoughts to me, watching as I took down every word in shorthand. I still cringe at the memory.

Politicians are wary and guileful for a good reason: journalists. And journalists interviewing politicians are probing and doubting for an equally good reason: those wary and guileful politicians. 'A culture of mutual contempt' is how John Williams, a former director of communications at the Foreign Office, who also worked for the *Evening Standard* and the *Mirror*, described the relationship. His greatest worry was the way both parties were despised by the public. Often the reason is that in far too many print and TV interviews the question that the journalists are asking themselves is: 'Why is this lying bastard lying to me?'

It's a question that's funny, pushy and carries with it an aura of superiority. It always gets a laugh – except from politicians. But is it wise? Certainly not when it can be described as 'knee-jerk cynicism'. Certainly not if, from the moment the journalist and the politician meet, there's an almost tangible hiss of 'liar, liar' in the air.

Former minister Michael Portillo, who in his time has been Secretary of State for Defence, Minister of State for Transport, Minister of State for Local Government and Inner Cities and Secretary of State for Employment, says: 'I very often felt like a prisoner in the dock. I was guilty and had to try and establish my innocence.'

Some politicians just sound as if they have something to hide. Charlie Brooker put it neatly in the *Guardian* 'Guide': there's 'the sort of politician who's programmed to avoid straight answers by default. Each time his brain approaches a straight answer, it's instantly repelled, as if by an opposing magnetic field.'

How would you react if endless interviewers presumed from the word go that you were lying? No surprise: you'd become wary and guileful. So why not make the interview pleasant? Many politicians respond well to interested and entertaining journalists. Query the truth of what they're telling you only if you have good grounds to do so.

And those occasions will arise, and you'll find yourself certain your interviewee is lying. It's best then to ask yourself if an aggressive, condescending frame of mind is likely to inspire you to ask questions that will prompt valuable answers. Maybe yes, but more likely no. It's wisest at this point not to go on the attack, but rather to adopt a more restrained approach and ask yourself: 'Why is this clever/troubled/powerful/ruthless/unhappy politician lying to me?' Such an attitude is geared towards encouraging you to adopt a more sympathetic and personal approach, asking genuinely curious questions, aimed to encourage valuable responses.

The classic 'conflict question'

Evasive politicians often have good reason for not wanting to answer certain questions, especially those to which, whatever they say, the reply won't look good. Psychologist Peter Bull, author of *The Micro-Analysis of Political Communication: Claptrap and Ambiguity*, offers this example: the question Jeremy Paxman asked Tony Blair on television about Iraq's 'weapons of mass destruction' and the suicide of Dr David Kelly, a senior defence scientist. The question was: 'Do you accept any responsibility, at all, for the death of Dr David Kelly?'

This, says Bull, is a classic 'conflict question'. However Blair responds to it, the consequences will be bad. If Blair says yes, he does accept some responsibility, it reflects badly on him and his government. If he says no, he accepts no responsibility at all, he looks careless and unfeeling.

So what does Blair do? 'He equivocates,' says Bull. Paxman repeats the question twice, eventually saying: 'It's a question to which you could give a yes or no answer.' And Blair replies: 'Yes, but it's maybe not a question you need to give a yes or no answer to.' Paxman changes the subject.

It does seem that approaches are changing slowly. TV interviewer Jeremy Vine has admitted having 'quite a high opinion' of politicians. Their job, he says, is fairly thankless, they probably could earn more elsewhere and they're 'treated like something the cat brought in'. He doesn't share the 'Why-is-this-lying-bastard-lying-to-me?' school of thought. 'If we believe that all politicians do is lie, then what is the point?' he asks.

'[The] insular, gossipy world of Westminster lends itself well to the medium of blogging, and several political journalists are now prolific in their online output,' says Daniel Forman of *The House* (the magazine for the Houses of Parliament). It's clear from blogs on the big daily newspapers' websites that national politics makes a rewarding and lively subject, one that journalists appear to enjoy writing – a few of them going to the extent of replying to some readers.

Back to the future

There is a theory that journalists' reputation hit rock bottom after Princess Diana's death because of the way the paparazzi had behaved. While complaints about accuracy continue to be aimed at journalists, news management is now so sophisticated that we should also question the role of PRs, says Peter Wilby in the *Guardian*. He describes press relations as 'the industry that [Alastair] Campbell temporarily joined when he worked for Blair'. Even Alastair Campbell has admitted that 'Perhaps we were over-controlling, manipulative. People stopped trusting what we had to say' – though he argued that this was partly the result of 'hostile and cynical media'.

All this means that, when interviewing politicians, journalists should follow the basic guidelines with extra care. Go in having done lots of detailed research, knowing exactly what you want to know, being prepared to listen more than talk and – here's where empathy becomes more important than ever – able to know what reaction your questions are likely to provoke.

To succeed at interviewing politicians it's valuable to go back and analyse the whole process, from the historical evolution of political interviews to learning how today's politicians see, use and try to control the media. First, remind yourself what the political interview is meant to represent. Even with today's technology, there's no way a politician, minister or local councillor can talk to all the voters. Historically, the journalist's role was to ask the searching questions that intelligent voters would ask if they had the chance.

Unfortunately, that has been distorted, as today's political journalists will testify. They regularly have to work through PRs, spin doctors, highly sophisticated news managers of all persuasions, so it's harder to question politicians effectively. However, it remains essential, because politics is one of the most important aspects of life and needs to be taken seriously. It's also one area where journalists can contribute to the democratic process.

Empathise

Harold Frayman, now on the *Guardian*, worked with politicians for more than 20 years. He says: 'The biggest problem for journalists trying to interview politicians is that most journalists can't put themselves in politicians' shoes. They can't empathise.' If they did, they might realise how hazardous being a politician can be.

Frayman compares politics with business, where you may be subject to a vicious campaign attacking what you're doing. Your customers may drift away but over time you have a chance to put things right. If people boycott your product, you can develop others. 'But politicians' customers vote on one occasion, all at one time,' Frayman says. 'All your opponent needs is a simple majority and then you haven't just lost that product, you've lost the world.'

Probably more than any other group, politicians feel under attack. They have good reason, being one of the least trusted groups in society; they're not considered to be caring or sincere. Yet, carrying this burden of public distrust and disapproval, they're obliged by law to publish details of decisions and transcripts of debates. As Frayman says:

> They have to do things in public, but they don't like it any more than anyone else would . . . The truth is that most politicians, however cynical, however ambitious, are motivated by a public interest more than a selfish interest. I'm not saying there's no self-interest, but they do want to do something positive. They do want to change the world for the better.

Lies, damn lies

Far too often, politicians are quizzed by badly briefed, poorly trained pushovers who waste everyone's precious time, but also by crusading reporters and feature writers determined to nail them with the old, old question resonating in their heads.

Yes, politicians do lie, but so do most people. There's nothing about being a politician that makes them naturally more inclined to be dishonest, but they end up stating as a fact what they actually hope will happen. To put it another way, politicians have a tendency to speak only partial truths, for 'politics would often be impossible without public reticence' – diplomatic language from former *Guardian* deputy editor John Cole.

When dealing with the press, politicians are aware, above all, of the vital importance of perception. They work energetically to project a positive image and never forget that, unless cleverly handled, careless comments may pitch them into a black hole. One serious gaffe can hold back advancement or, at worst, destroy a career – less easily now, perhaps, but it happens. More than almost any group, they know the value of publicity and the power of the media.

Respect wanes

First, a look at how politicians have been treated in this country in the lifetime of present MPs – a deliberately chosen timeframe. Though politicians couldn't survive if they didn't adapt to changing circumstances, there's no doubt they instinctively react well to approaches they feel comfortable with, and vice versa. For example, a man who turns up to give evidence to a specialised select committee but doesn't wear a tie mystifies many of them, and it's seen by some as an insult, not realising that to others it's fashionable.

'Is there anything else you'd like to tell the nation, prime minister?' was the deferential approach many years ago. By the 1950s, though still treating politicians with respect, journalists began to ask more pertinent questions and receive more carefully thought-out answers. The sharper questions of the 1960s resulted in fuller answers, and fuller answers led to more probing and forceful questions. It was probably the powerful reporting in the 1970s of the Watergate scandal in the United States – which forced President Nixon's resignation – coupled with the arrival of the *Sun* in Britain, that heralded the beginning of the end of press deference. On TV, interviews became deliberately adversarial; in print, they became tougher and rougher.

By the 1980s, with Margaret Thatcher as prime minister, politicians had learnt from the United States. The number of press officers nearly doubled and consultants were hired to advise on everything from hairstyles to hand movements (or in Thatcher's case teeth and voice pitch), from when to lie low to when to schmooze, from when to attack to when to make pre-emptive confessions.

Politicians grew even more adept in the late 1990s when Alastair Campbell became Tony Blair's chief press secretary. 'He turned the aide's legitimate role of getting the best possible press for his employer into a high art of media manipulation,' says Peter Wilby. Campbell 'hugely extended the practice of trailing government announcements in advance, leaking them only partially so that they were reported in terms that suited his masters'. Campbell was rated Spin Doctor Supreme, and political journalist Michael Cockerell instanced an early example of Campbell's 'presentational skills' on the day after New Labour had won.

> Tony Blair and Alastair Campbell had flown down from Sedgefield and arrived just before daybreak at the Festival Hall, where the Labour celebrations were still in full swing. The climax would be the arrival of the victorious leader. But Campbell held Blair's car back out of sight. He was leaving nothing to chance with the grand entrance.
>
> He had phoned the meteorological office to find the exact moment that dawn would break and on cue he waved the Blairmobile forward. As Campbell later confided, there was no point in the Prime Minister-elect making a speech about the dawn of a new age in the dark.

Campbell could also be tough. 'You have only to sit as I have done in the Blair helicopter during an election campaign and watch Campbell lean over to slash out great sections of his leader's prepared remarks for the next venue,' said Robin Oakley.

Wilby concludes that PR is now infinitely more powerful, and that 'at least half the news in papers is generated not by journalists but by PRs or spin doctors, and very little is subject to serious critical scrutiny.

PR, far more than journalism, shapes the news agenda. And governments, big companies, well-funded pressure groups and wealthy individuals can afford more and better PR than anybody else.'

On that gloomy note, let's look at John Williams's judgement, the result of having been both a journalist and communications director at the Foreign Office. 'Having worked on both sides, I am convinced that each trade has the other badly wrong. Too many on each side regard the other as incapable of being straight, to the extent that the public trusts neither.'

The problem, he believes, is 'not the media's carelessness with facts, but relentless corrosion of the public's belief that ministers can be capable of acting in good faith, with basic competence and, occasionally, real achievement.'

He concludes: 'You cannot have democracy without both good government and good journalism. Ours has more of both than either side realises, and more than the public suspects. A culture of mutual contempt serves nobody's interest.' Amen to that. There's already encouraging news from the 2008 Orwell Prize (for political writing), which attracted a record number of entries including dozens judged to display 'courage, insight and honesty'.

Fresh thinking

By a process of natural selection, today's politicians are fit and equipped with the attributes and techniques necessary to defend themselves against the assaults of an aggressive press. Few other interviewees today are so skilful and need such a careful, well-planned approach.

It's important to understand the way they think, which is not how journalists think. Most journalists' priority is to cover facts, comments and quotes. Politicians' priority is to achieve the result they seek.

Just as it's hard for journalists to understand politicians, it's often difficult for politicians to understand journalists. They don't seem to realise that if you don't want people to know something, the best way is not to tell them. 'They think they can win favours', says one commentator, 'by passing on little titbits just for you and are astonished when they start turning up in print.'

The question they ask themselves

The question politicians ask themselves when being interviewed is: 'How will my words play in print?' Their most precious asset is how much they know. Information is power and they are on the inside. Robin Corbett, a former journalist, former MP for Birmingham Erdington and now Lord Corbett, put it succinctly when asked why he's not worried about being caught out by journalists: 'I usually know far more about the subject than they do.'

For MPs and many peers, politics is their life and their business, one conducted for much of the time person-to-person, face-to-face, in areas of Parliament or the local council chambers where journalists can't roam at will. Also, politicians are by nature adept manoeuvrers, adroit at side-stepping, ducking and weaving – skills they refine after endless practice at selection committees, party events, debates, meetings, meetings, meetings, interviews, interviews, interviews.

Because they're supremely outcome-oriented, they analyse the results of these meetings and interviews, learning all the time, tweaking and perfecting their responses. They learn to be close observers, acute judges of human nature and quick on the uptake.

Buffers and bruisers

With the emergence of spin doctors, politicians have become even harder to reach. It's useful for politicians to have someone who will stand between them and the journalists and do the shouting, which they perceive to be necessary.

With an experienced politician, all these defences are in place before a single journalist's question is asked. It's only then that they activate their formidable interview techniques, which for some include 30 different ways of not answering the question without refusing to do so point blank or else rephrasing it better to suit what they want to say (see page 43).

But first, who's up against them in this apparently unequal contest? At national daily paper level, the contest is not quite so unequal. Specialists such as lobby correspondents, gallery reporters, political editors and reporters covering areas like labour relations, health and education are often journalists with years of experience, who talk to politicians of every party at every level. Politicians, combative by nature, enjoy sparring with these experts, to whom politics is exciting and supremely important.

National reporters have the advantage that they can parcel out contact with politicians to suit themselves. If a particular reporter gets on well with one minister, that's fine. And if that minister tells their contact a story they shouldn't, well, the contact can pass it on so that it appears under a different by-line.

Style and substance

Unless you're on radio or TV, don't model your style on John Humphrys or Jeremy Paxman. The dynamics of interviewing for print are different. TV thrives on conflict. The politicians have agreed to appear and have most likely cleared the subjects they will be questioned on. Radio thrives on quick-fire exchange.

For print you should adopt a more subtle approach. The interviewers politicians dislike are the poorly prepared, the lazy, the untrained. The late Sir Robin Day, who'd spent a lifetime obsessed with interviews, put it neatly in his memoirs: 'Politicians like vigorous, well-informed questions. Training and experience make them responsive to such questioning. A limp, flabby and ill-informed interview does not stimulate them.'

Robin Corbett says: 'The worst are the bone idle, the ones who haven't done their homework, the sort who'd walk in and ask: "Are you a member of any committee, Mr Corbett?"' (In the Commons, he was chairman of the powerful Home Affairs Select Committee.) 'Or they don't know about local transport campaigns that we've been running for years. I go mad about it.'

He says that some of the worst offenders are on weekly papers, and he questions their induction process. He doesn't expect trainee reporters to be local experts immediately, but says it's important that they find out what's going on in the district: who's the largest local employer, what local concerns are, and so on.

'They don't know the local councillors or where they drink. Papers are run like fire stations: reporters leave only when the alarm bells ring.' There are stories everywhere, right on their doorstep, he says, if only reporters would look – though he recognises the pressures under which they work. This is where keen trainees and journalists who are happy to put in extra hours score, though admittedly by agreeing to be exploited.

Techniques for journalists

Politicians are generally astute, informed and motivated, and will gladly tell you what they want you to know. The skill is enticing them to tell what they'd rather you *didn't* know, either now, later, or ever. The journalist usually knows what the politician's message is likely to be and will have heard it before. The politician suspects, often correctly, that the journalist doesn't want to hear it again.

Politicians may try to throw you or make you feel uncomfortable, but that's unlikely at a first meeting. Then they are likely to take your measure. The advice from a government press officer who for several years sat in on ministerial interviews is: 'Know your stuff. Politicians, whatever party, don't want to be interviewed by fools who haven't done their homework. They can tell from the first few questions what the journalist's agenda is and how clued up they are.'

His advice is to let politicians ramble on a little at first and listen to what they say – in order, first, to accord them recognition of their position; second, to be able to ask supplementary questions. Certainly, he advises, never reveal your own politics.

The really adroit political journalist, he says, knows who each politician is friendly with and who they sit next to in the House of Commons or House of Lords. 'I like politicians because it's such a clever profession, so skilful,' he says. 'They know they're powerful and that it doesn't go on for ever. It's all about presentation, acting, putting on a show.'

Far too many young journalists, he says, put on dismal performances. 'I'm astounded by the stupidity of some young reporters: so ill-informed I wonder how they are ever going to write a story about anything.'

Softly, softly

'Putting politicians at their ease is not simple,' according to a political adviser, 'because if they're any good at being a politician they're not going to relax.' Start with simple questions that they find easy to answer.

Politicians are no exception to that rule, though asking how they spell their names is not a good idea. Checking might be permissible with parish councillors or candidates from obscure parties, but not otherwise.

Local paper trainee reporters should set out to establish a good relationship with their local MPs right away. Remember that almost every politician you talk to will be an experienced interviewee and won't be impressed if you arrive late, haven't brought a pen or forget to carry spare batteries for your recorder.

Your immediate imperative is to get the story, and your first objective should be to convince them of your ability to report accurately. You'll get more if you sound as though you are basically in tune with what they are saying. Being combative just reminds them that the chances are the interview could do them damage.

That doesn't mean you gush enthusiastically when being told of their plans for improving litter bins, but it does mean you show that you are listening and understand what they're saying. Ask intelligent questions be they Conservative, Labour, Liberal Democrat, Green, Scottish National Party, UKIP (United Kingdom Independence Party) or – should you find yourself interviewing one of them – the elusive Monster Raving Loony Party.

The last party, likely now to be found lurking around parish council elections (much cheaper than standing for Parliament) is included because some of its original proposals have since become law: for example, reducing the voting age from 21 to 18; pedestrianising Carnaby Street in London; and all-day opening of pubs.

A sympathetic, understanding response often produces a better result than direct questioning. Saying, 'Yes, and I suppose . . .' shows that you understand what they are driving at. It reassures them, too, which is very important during early interviews, because being misunderstood and misquoted is a standard fear.

If your reports are accurate, they will remember and should be happy to talk to you again. After one or two more meetings they may offer you something fairly tempting 'off the record'. If you want them to trust you – and it's very much in your interest that they do – it's important to establish that you both understand exactly what that means: information 'off the record' is something you agree not to print.

If they won't change it to 'unattributable' – information you can print but without identifying the source – then either switch off the recorder, put down your pen or make a big, black mark in your notebook indicating what is 'off the record'. When you type back your notes, put that info on a separate page, store it separately and *don't* print it.

Gaining trust is like a ritual mating dance. It takes time and is neither easily established nor lightly given. Protestations by the journalist, such as 'You can trust me – I won't tell a soul', are counter-productive, since they give the opposite impression. Report accurately and don't betray confidences. That builds trust.

But what happens when trust is so successful that you genuinely become friends? This can be difficult, says Andrew Marr. 'If you don't form close understandings with senior politicians, so that you can hear them think aloud, honestly, in a relaxed way, then you are unlikely to understand much of what is really going on. Yet if you do, then you drift closer to them emotionally and may very well flinch from putting the boot in when they have failed in some way.'

Marr believes that the solution is for the 'honest' journalist to behave like a shit – 'build up close sources and then, quite often, betray them'. Marr recalls an example. 'He never forgave me, cutting me dead for years. He was right, too.'

Follow up

Robin Corbett's advice for all non-specialist reporters who deal with politicians, besides do your homework, is: follow up what you're told. 'I can count on the fingers of one hand the number of times in 25 years in the Commons that reporters have actually followed up comments such as "I'm so upset about this I'm going to write to the prime minister." All it takes is a phone call and one question: "What happened?"'

Local paper reporters are particularly well placed to be fed with excellent stories if they show they understand politicians and their priorities. But why should MPs bother with an untrained reporter, whose previous interview was a waste of time, when a well-written press release would: (a) be more accurate; (b) probably be printed almost in its entirety; and (c) would save them time and trouble? The obvious answer is that they need to be elected and keep in contact with the press, who can help or harm them. They know that the press can be vindictive if slighted or scorned. So requests for interviews will be turned down with sadness and the hope there'll be time in the future – which will arrive nearer election time.

How *not* to interview politicians

Straight after she had been selected as the Conservative Party's candidate for the Battersea constituency, Jane Ellison was interviewed by a relatively young journalist whose first question was: 'Are you one of Cameron's babes?'

'Laughable' is how Ellison sums up the question. 'If the journalist had done any research at all,' she says, 'she'd have known how long I had been in the party and that I had fought for seats in such down-to-earth places as Barnsley, Tottenham and Pendle' (a Lancashire borough made up of five towns: Nelson, Colne, Brierfield, Barnoldswick and Earby). 'And also – at 40-something – I wasn't anyone's babe.' So, first message: you must do your research.

Though her reaction to this first question was that she had no wish to spend much time with the journalist, Ellison recognises that 'a good follow-up question could have redeemed her'. So what was the next question? 'Are you a member of the Notting Hill set?' This, says Ellison, is 'batty', because she works for a major retail company (the John Lewis Partnership) and has a 'reasonably obvious northern accent'.

Her reaction was immediate. By this time, she says, she had no faith that the journalist was going to ask anything intelligent. She neatly diagnosed the journalist's mistake: she was using a 'one-size-fits-all' list of questions. So, second message: design your questions specifically for your interviewee.

Interestingly – bearing in mind the 'Why is this lying bastard lying to me?' attitude of journalists – Ellison thinks that a few of them are not completely straight with her. They give hard-to-believe reasons why they want to come and talk to her in Battersea. It's not because, she says, that way they will get a representative sample of views in a marginal seat – after all, the famous Northcote Road in Battersea is not representative – but because it's convenient. 'I think I sometimes get calls because I'm nearby and time is short, but I don't mind if they say that!' she says.

She also – engagingly – admits that in the past she has on occasion avoided telling the truth in response to some questions in places like Barnsley, an ultra-safe Labour seat.

When asked if she expected to win, she didn't say: 'No, I expect to lose', because, she says: 'It's only fair on those people who are working hard on your campaign.' She didn't want to demoralise them, so she did her best to say something positive and true at the same time.

Distractions

Being pushed too much by journalists makes politicians jumpy. Feeling under attack can trigger exactly the reaction the journalist doesn't want: up go the defences. For any chance to succeed you need to be aware of the defence techniques they may use.

If your questions approach an area they don't want to discuss, distractions include:

- the red herring (a diverting – in both senses – snippet of information dangled enticingly before the journalist's nose);
- the putdown (a barely disguised insult designed to wrong-foot the journalist and put them on the defensive);
- word-bridging and looping (smoothly slipping away from a subject they don't want to discuss onto one they do – demonstrated nearly every morning on Radio 4's Today programme);
- the steamroller (carrying on regardless of question, interjection, raised pen, raised eyebrows, any attempt by interviewer to speak);
- 'I'm glad you asked me that' (precursor to a long-winded explanation that goes absolutely nowhere);
- treats and titbits (rewards for good behaviour – beware, they usually come with a price tag attached);
- a flat refusal (much the hardest to combat).

'But answer came there none . . .'

Politicians avoid answering difficult questions in countless ways but their ploys break down into nine main categories, with at least three times that number of variants. The main categories are to:

- ignore the question;
- acknowledge the question without answering it;
- question the question;
- attack the question;
- decline to answer;
- make a political point, for example by attacking an opponent;
- give an incomplete answer;
- repeat a previous answer;
- claim to have answered the question already.

These findings come from research on television interviews carried out by Dr Peter Bull and Kate Mayer of York University. They also logged comments when interviewers interrupted in order to ask another question. These responses included:

- 'No, please let me go on';
- 'May I just finish';
- 'One moment';
- 'I must beg of you';
- 'Please may I';
- 'Let me finish it';
- 'Can I just finish it';
- 'Will you give me time';
- 'May I say something else';
- 'May I now and then say a word in my own defence';
- 'Please may I say';
- 'But can I just go on';
- 'Yes, but one moment';
- 'Please, there's just one other thing';
- 'One moment, hold on';
- 'No, don't stop me'.

If politicians use these tactics on television against formidable interviewers, imagine how they relish novice print interviewers.

The point is that politicians need to get their message across to the voters, who seldom read party manifestos (alas, many journalists don't either). So because politicians need the potential publicity from political interviews, they regularly turn interviews into rants and try to bulldoze or steamroller. They forget that bulldozers and steamrollers can't cope with hilly terrain, get stuck at the foot of deep valleys and sink into mud.

Local government

Local politicians representing the largest and most powerful cities and counties can be every bit as tricky as MPs. Indeed, many MPs start in local government. Local politicians representing the smaller counties, cities and boroughs may have more limited back-up facilities but can be formidable too. Sadly, changed rules relating to local government and the appalling pressure under which many reporters now work mean that there is less opportunity for them to attend council meetings – and rarely enough time to sit there right to the end. Add this to the falling circulations and declining ad incomes of some local newspapers and the wolves are on the prowl.

The threat that some local newspapers face comes from their local councils. Indeed, as this book is being written, there is a move – certainly in London – for councils to make their monthly magazines larger and more frequent, with an eye on increased income from advertising.

'Local newspaper bosses should stop bleating about the rising tide of quality council newspapers and start reflecting on some hard truths facing the industry,' says Simon Jones, head of communications at Hammersmith and Fulham Council. He believes that the local press has only itself to blame.

'Check with the press office ...'

Requests for interviews with members of staff are now almost always first directed to the press office. The result is that far too many papers make do by printing speedily edited city, county or borough press releases which neatly spin the local line. Bad, bad, bad. Do your very best to persuade the news editor to build in time for you to attend important meetings. There is nothing like reporting what's actually said in meetings to control councillors. For novice reporters, the best ones to interview are the newly elected local councillors who have almost everything to learn.

Though local politicians' status may be lower, the need for journalists to be accurate is as great; and so is the irritation experienced by misquoted local politicians. This is primarily because they live and work close to their voters, whereas many Westminster MPs can trudge round their constituencies largely unrecognised.

Gain their trust

Advice for local journalists is, in effect, a council of perfection: attend meetings as much as possible, frequent pubs, work the phones, talk to the politicians, gain their trust. Aim for stories, not rewritten press releases, at regular intervals.

On the other side of local government are the officials – a mixed group. Some are stars in their own right, some tediously self-important, some of them delighted to be interviewed and talk about their work. The only given is, do your research first.

A long-time freelance told me she'd only once had to adopt a 'Silly Little Me privileged to talk to Mr Knowledgeable You' stance for an interview, and that was with a south London borough official. The interview related to catering outlets in the area and, after the usual preliminaries, it went along the following lines:

> Freelance: 'I'm writing a feature about . . . and it seems to me [trotting out her research findings]. Am I right that . . .?'
>
> Official: 'Wrong. Rubbish.'
>
> Freelance: 'Well . . .'
>
> Official: 'You're like all journalists, think you know everything.'
>
> Freelance: 'No, I don't. That's why I'm here, so . . .'
>
> Official: 'You know absolutely nothing. I've met people like you before. Come in here, thinking you know everything when you know nothing. I've spent . . . years in local government, man and boy, and I know every inch of the borough. This is your first visit here, isn't it?' [It wasn't, but she let it go.]
>
> Freelance (alerted by the 'man and boy' clue): 'Mr . . ., that's why I'm here. To get the facts right. To talk to someone who knows all about it, so I don't make any stupid mistakes. I'd really appreciate as much help as you can give me. I know how important it is to get the facts from an expert.'
>
> Official (slightly mollified): 'Well, at least you've come to the right person. I know what you need to know, so you'd better listen.'

And she did. 'I played up to it, though I hated it. I'd like to report that he was awful, but the truth is that, with his ego massaged by dollops of wow and gosh and my goodness, he gave me a good interview.'

Hunting as a pack

All too often at press conferences journalists concentrate on the questions they want to ask or the questions the news desk has told them to ask and ignore one of the great interviewing guidelines: listen to the answers.

When journalists listen and are able to ask follow-up questions, they often get a better story. But the more experienced try to save their questions until they can talk to the politician later, privately. That's how exclusives happen.

Journalists at press conferences are there to get a story, not to help anyone else, so working together is rare. But when it happens and they decide to hunt in a pack, the result can be devastating.

Harold Frayman remembers a Conservative Party Central Office general election press conference with Mrs Thatcher, an acknowledged expert at not answering the question. 'General election press conferences are very formal set pieces,' says Frayman, 'and they have to finish at a set time.' This is because the next party press conference which the political journalists plan to attend is scheduled to begin x minutes later and timing is vital for journalists to meet media deadlines.

> Tony Bevins, then at the *Express*, asked a question that Mrs Thatcher really did not want to answer. She smiled and said 'That's a very interesting question,' and turned to another journalist and said 'Bill . . .?"
>
> Usually everyone's got questions they want to ask on their own account, and this would have worked most times, but on this occasion Bill said: 'Actually, the question I would most like answered is the one Tony just asked you.'
>
> Mrs Thatcher grinned and said 'Don't be silly', then turned to someone else and that someone else said, 'Ah, yes. Now what I'd like to ask you is the question Tony asked.' And for once – and it really was a once – the press pack ganged up instead of fighting individually and the truth was that it worked. She had to answer the question. She couldn't keep on turning it aside.
>
> Most press conferences go the way of the person running them. If there were more working together in press conferences there'd be more chance of getting answers.

Working together like this is so rare that, when it happens, journalists present recollect it years later in their memoirs. At least 30 years after the event, Alistair Cooke in *Six Men* graphically recalled how American presidential hopeful Henry Wallace was asked whether he'd written a series of rather strange letters obtained by an opponent (Westbrook Pegler) and printed in a hostile publication over Wallace's signature. Wallace answered that he 'never discussed Westbrook Pegler'. He was asked four more times – once by Pegler – and made the same reply.

Then the famous journalist H. L. Mencken – the P. J. O'Rourke of his time – asked Wallace: 'Would you consider me a Pegler stooge?' After the laughter subsided, Wallace replied, 'No, Mr Mencken, I would never consider you anybody's stooge.' So Mencken continued:

> Well, then, it's a simple question. We've all written love letters in our youth that bring a blush later on. There's no shame in it. This is a question that all of us here would like to have answered, so we can move on to weightier things.

Wallace made no answer, leaving listeners, as Cooke concludes, to draw the obvious conclusion.

Poacher-turned-gamekeeper Robin Corbett knows the tricks of both trades. He handles press conferences when he wants to be quoted by offering the press soundbites. 'You don't need to tip a million words over people. I say it all in three sentences and shut up.' And he makes sure he speaks vividly and in pictures.

The converse of this is true – when politicians *don't* want to be quoted they talk at great length, in a dreary, monotonous voice, and waffle or ramble on. That's when concentrated listening becomes even more important.

Making contact

MPs are easy to contact and in great demand; members of the House of Lords somewhat less so, yet they present huge potential. 'We're stuffed with experts,' says (Lord) Corbett. Some of these are promoted MPs who bring with them to the Lords expertise they developed during their time in the Commons. Others have been ennobled because of their special skills. To check potential interviewees try the register of lords' interests.

Be warned: some lords are difficult to reach because they prefer not to publicise their email addresses, so, to reach them, it's best to write or telephone.

Press Gazette's gossip columnist noted that two journalists working together regularly interviewed senior and aged politicians in the Lords. 'Those on the red benches were so enamoured and enthralled that two young, attractive journalists paid them so much attention, that they would often spill the beans' – and as a result the journalists secured several scoops, and, later, excellent jobs.

Think about it.

10 Interviewing celebrities

Some journalists are so desperate to interview celebrities that they'll agree to nearly everything the PRs demand. That can include writer approval, question approval, copy approval, photographer approval, picture approval and/or clothes approval.

'Why not save yourself the hassle and just get them to write the piece for you instead?' says Gill Hudson, *Radio Times* editor. 'You'll get exactly the same kind of coma-inducing copy anyway.' Then she offers another option. It takes some effort, she says – it's journalism.

What follows is a selection of some of Britain's most able journalists talking about interviewing celebrities. It becomes clear that one approach doesn't fit all. The answer is not black and white but more like infinite shades of grey, as the journalists work out approaches that suit them, their brief and their interviewees.

Consider this: three experienced, talented journalists offer their solutions to a problem that often occurs if you are interviewing a celebrity known to have a very touchy skeleton in their cupboard.

Do you raise the subject at all, early in the interview, halfway through, three-quarters of the way or at the very end?

Emma Brockes, who writes for the *Guardian* and the *New York Times*, believes 'It's bad to wait till the last five minutes, blurt out "Did you hate your dad?" and then leg it out of the room. Ideally, she says, it should come three-quarters of the way through, when you've still got a bit of time.'

Lynn Barber, in her magnificent introduction to *Mostly Men*, her book of collected interviews (see page 234), opts for 'asking early and boldly, accepting the answer and then getting on with the interview.

The subject's relief at having survived it so quickly and painlessly may pay dividends for the rest of the interview.'

Andrew Duncan, who writes exclusively for *Radio Times*, will 'adopt one of several approaches' (see page 154).

The truth is, there's no one rule here that works for such complex interviews. In fact, the word 'rule' is rarely used in this book. 'Guidance' is preferred. The recommended approach here is one that works best for the individual journalist, based on their temperament and their assessment of their interviewee.

Let's start by checking whether you're ready for celebrities. My advice is to put in a substantial amount of face-to-face interviewing before launching yourself into the showbiz world. You need to be completely at ease with the process and be ready to do lots of research. It helps if you're interested in psychology and body language and work for a successful paper or magazine. It also helps if you're naturally persuasive, persistent, confident and enthusiastic.

A sellers' market

First, it's important that you take great care when making requests for celebrity interviews. Present yourself and your publication as favourably as possible and work out why it should be in their interest to talk to you.

'Journalists today are buyers in a sellers' market and a market which gets tougher all the time,' says Lynn Barber. Perceptive, witty and unafraid, she puts the case for celebrity interviewing better than anyone else. She appears throughout this chapter: first, offering advice – passionately held – relating to the early stages. Second, with details of how she interviews. Do read her books *Mostly Men* and *Demon Barber*, particularly for their forewords.

She admits she admires people who have the drive to become famous, and is very curious about the effect fame has on people, but she *never interviews from the knees*. Far from it. She knows you can't be a fan and an interviewer at the same time.

Journalists almost always now deal through PRs who usually work for the film or show producer, not for the celebrity. The PR's job is to get as much publicity for the 'product' as possible. That explains this steely message from Harrison Ford.

> I'm here to transfer information. I'm here for no other reason than to bring this film to the public's attention. Actors and journalists have a symbiotic relationship. I'm here to serve you as long as you're here to serve me. I'm not here to become famous, I'm not here to have myths made about me. I'm here to help define your understanding of what I do and why I do it, which may have something new to offer people who have spent 20 years listening to the same crap.

'The celeb wars have got worse,' says Barber. There are now more magazines and papers 'chasing essentially the same number of stars'. One consequence is that PRs have so much power that they can – and do – ban journalists who write anything they consider unpleasant.

When it comes to the interview, Barber insists that the ability *not* to talk about yourself is essential. 'The good interviewer is faceless, ego-less, devoid of personality,' she says; the personality can come into the writing.

She's also insistent about how best to start an interview. She castigates those who want to make friends, who want to be liked, who want a conversation or the start of a beautiful friendship. 'You don't have to make friends, you don't have to express opinions, you only have to ask questions,' she says.

In *Mostly Men* she says she begins by asking a long, clever, scripted question. This, she says, is a way of saying she's read all the cuttings and expects that they will make an effort. She adds: 'There is also a faint hope that, by showing my familiarity with all their previous interviews, I can prevent them giving me the same old guff they've given before, though the hope often proves illusory.'

That gives you some idea of the journalist's work – but what about the celebrity? Novelist Nadine Gordimer says questions are so predictable that she and anybody else regularly interviewed could reply in their sleep. After being interviewed by more than 30 journalists in one day, Julia Roberts told Chris Heath of the *Independent on Sunday* that she was so bored that, when a Japanese journalist asked if there was anything in the film which the Japanese might relate to, she sighed and said: 'I wouldn't have the foggiest idea.'

The editor-in-chief of a successful women's magazine says: 'Generally, the more famous the star is, the easier the whole project will be – it's those nearer to the Z-list who cause the most trouble,' which is bad news for beginner journalists – or could it be rated as the best training ever?

George Stiles has been interviewed all round the world about the songs he writes, most famously the new ones for the hit stage musical of *Mary Poppins*, and the Olivier Award-winning *Honk!* which has been seen on every continent by a total of more than six million people.

He's a very experienced interviewee and remembers vividly the worst interview he ever suffered – and suffer is the word. He and Richard Sherman, who wrote the songs for the *Mary Poppins* film, were interviewed together by a 'rank amateur' – an interviewer whose only desire was to show off how much he knew; how his father had stimulated his interest in musicals; how his father had encouraged his song writing; how clever he was . . . he, himself . . . on and on.

But that wasn't all. When he stopped talking about himself he concentrated totally on Richard Sherman, who he lionised. 'I was ready for this,' Stiles says. 'I was sitting next to a multi-Oscar-winning songwriter, a legend in his 70s.' Sherman tried to steer the discussion back to Stiles and the new songs, but with little success. 'In the end I think I was asked one question and sat there for 45 minutes for the privilege.'

By contrast, what does this experienced songwriter look for in interviews? First, journalists who are well prepared. If they've done their research, he finds he warms to them. He also says interviewers should come across as happy to be there and never give the impression that they're doing anyone a favour.

Stiles suggests journalists should 'blow a bit of smoke. Say you saw the musical the previous night, or had seen it before and enjoyed it – or at least that you'd read the press release.' He also likes it when they get going fast; it's no surprise that, with his long experience of being interviewed and being asked the same things nearly all the time, he's delighted when surprised by fresh and surprising questions. 'Interviewing is a mini relationship,' Stiles says. 'And it can be flirtatious.'

So, what's the best interview he remembers? Again it was with Richard Sherman, but how different. It was held in a Manhattan studio where such legends as Ella Fitzgerald had recorded. The two journalists were wonderfully prepared and there was a piano in the room. It made all the difference. 'When you interview composers like this,' says Stiles, 'you get a wonderful sense that they are in their element. We both opened up, able to demonstrate what we do.'

The resulting published interview reflected all the joy of the music the guys had heard and was a fresh, wonderful piece. For journalists working exclusively with and through the written word, this is a vital approach that we neglect to our real loss.

Finally, what's it like being interviewed for a whole day by a stream of journalists, 99.9 per cent of whom ask exactly the same questions? 'Absolutely knackering,' says Stiles.

Differing styles

Of the interviewers who deserve to be taken seriously, there are two sorts: those who interview celebrities and those who are 'celebrity interviewers'. Emma Brockes is one of the first, Andrew Duncan and Lynn Barber two of the second.

Because most celebrities are plugging something, Barber lets them plug it early and often at length, listening carefully for their turn of phrase, pitch and speed of speaking. This means she can later pick up any telltale hesitation or glibness.

She's in favour of getting her interviewee talking and says the best question is the shortest one that will unlock the longest answer. She also knows tough questioning usually produces good quotes. By contrast with the *Sunday Times* interviewer who asked politician Harriet Harman, 'Would you call yourself an intellectual?', Barber asked her, 'Are you thick?' She knows that when people have to defend themselves to someone who is genuinely interested in them, they often produce passionate and printable answers.

She admits her 'thick' question sounds ruder. Correct, but I would bet she asked it in a way that didn't give offence. She knows that the really deadly questions are the dulcet ones. I'm also sure she never asked the 'thick' question until she was certain Harman knew how very interested she was in what Harman had to say.

Finally, she says she's a better interviewer now than she was when young and pretty. On flirting she says:

> You don't *need* sexual chemistry, when the chemistry of taking an intense, informed interest in someone is so potent. There are very few people in the world who can resist the opportunity to talk about themselves at length to someone who seems genuinely, deeply interested and who has obviously thought about (i.e. read up) their life beforehand.

The art of seduction

Suzie Mackenzie, writing for the *Guardian*, calls interviewing 'the art of practised seduction', and admits to using every wile.

> You're going to smile, to laugh at their jokes, give them every possible sign that they have your complete attention – that, when they look into your eyes, the person you are seeing is the person they want you to see. But interviewing is not about charming someone, it's to do with making them want to charm you and then not resisting their charm.

Andrew Billen admits that 'the one time I subsequently had a proper relationship with one of my subjects, I discovered that almost everything she had told me on the record had contained a lie of commission or omission.' He, too, admits to worrying much more about the potential two-facedness of interviewers. 'Once you've said goodbye there's no professional obligation to maintain in print the sympathetic smile with which you received an indiscretion.' You can twist, editorialise, boost, belittle.

Like Lynn Barber he justifies his decisions by saying that, if there is any honour in interviewing, it must lie in the relationship between the interviewer and the reader. 'When someone asks me what so-and-so was really like, I always reply that I have tried to answer exactly that question in my piece.'

The cynical view is that a typical showbiz interview is like a rendezvous with a hooker. Xan Brooks in *The Big Issue* wrote: 'You meet in an anonymous hotel room. You have an allotted time together. All too often the interviewee doesn't know who you are or where you come from. The subject provides basic information (well-worn anecdotes passed off as revelations) while the questioner fishes pathetically for something more deep and lasting.'

Barry Norman, a showbiz writer for the *Daily Mail* before turning to television, and now back with *Radio Times*, says it's very important to put stars at ease – often more difficult than it might sound.

> Movie stars usually have a kind of tunnel vision – which is understandable. They're in a precarious position because there are always people younger and prettier and probably better actors – movie stardom and acting rarely go together – coming along behind them.

One approach, he says, is to start by asking: 'How did this film come about? What's your involvement?' Then, you know you'll get something you can use. 'It might not be terribly fascinating but it's a good icebreaker and gets them talking.'

British actors are easier to interview than Hollywood stars, says Norman.

> Very few of them get huge money and they've usually had to struggle. Overnight success for the average British actor takes 10 years and they remember it. They remember when they were poor, scurrying round trying to find another small speaking part in a TV play.
>
> Big movie stars forget quickly that they were once poor. They're surrounded with bodyguards and it makes them feel important. Their entourage are telling them all the time how marvellous, how wonderful they are, and they believe it.

As far as ploys go, Norman knows the power of silence.

> If a guy has told you something which he knows is not the whole truth, or only part of the truth, and you sit there and look at him and let five or 10 seconds go by, he will almost certainly start explaining further and you're getting close to the kind of stuff you really want. But it takes some nerve. Don't be afraid.

He's alert to counter-ploys. 'When they start using little tricks you know it's because they are trying to evade the real issue.' Take leg crossing: 'If an attractive woman is doing it, it may mean she's trying to distract your attention from what you're asking. "Hang on," you think, "there's something in these questions she doesn't want to talk about."'

Norman's rule is to interview only those stars, writers and directors whose work he likes. 'I don't see any point in giving free publicity to rubbish.'

CASE STUDY 4 – EMMA BROCKES TALKS TO EMMA LEE-POTTER

Emma Brockes is an award-winning journalist. She was named Young Journalist of the Year at the British Press Awards in 2001 and scooped Feature Writer of the Year in 2002. During 10 years as a staff writer at the *Guardian*, she interviewed everyone from Liza Minnelli to Madeleine Albright. Now freelance and based in New York, she writes for the *Guardian* and the *New York Times*.

These days most national newspapers use dedicated 'fixers' to set up celebrity interviews, and the *Guardian* is no exception. Brockes says that this seemed an 'extraordinary luxury' when she first joined the paper, but it is actually more efficient and saves time. She still, however, fixes other interviews herself.

'I will write a personal letter and try to make the case that I am the best person there is in the competition to interview them – either because I have some special interest in the subject or perhaps by some quirk of background that might win their sympathy. You have to try and get them to think of you as a real person and make a connection with them.'

For two years Brockes wrote a major weekly interview for the *Guardian*'s G2 section. It was crucial to plan and prepare properly. 'It would take a morning probably, or at the very most a day. If there was a book to read then I would read it the night before. You can over-prepare, though. The key to preparation isn't reading thousands and thousands of other pieces, it's sitting and trying to think about the best way into the difficult areas of this person's life.'

Rather than preparing a long list of questions, Brockes concentrates on plotting a route through the interview, from the beginning to the end. In particular, she works out 'key turning points' in advance – moments in the interview where she hopes to move from the publicity guff that celebrities want her to talk about and onto the juicy stuff.

'I find that there is always a conversion question that changes the atmosphere of the interview,' she says. 'In a way, it's like getting a rocket into re-entry. If you get the angle of entry wrong you just whizz off into outer space and there is no getting back.

'The best example I can think of was when I interviewed Charlize Theron just after she won an Oscar for best actress in *Monster* in 2004. She had already been interviewed by about 30 hacks in the morning and I only had 20 minutes with her. She was encased in make-up, having done a load of shoots, and the whole thing felt ridiculous and contrived. I knew that within those 20 minutes I had to get the conversation round to how her mother had shot her father dead when she was 15. One journalist from a Durban newspaper had said to her: "So, Charlize, in this film you play a serial killer called Aileen Wuornos. Your mum killed your dad – that must have been a good insight." She just said "It's not the same" and shut the interview down.

'I thought for hours about how to approach this with her. After we chatted about the film and the Oscar for a bit, I said: "Do you wish your dad was still alive to see you win the Oscar?" "Of course I do," she said. "I wouldn't wish something like that on anybody. Nobody deserves that." And then you're in. You know that she doesn't hate him. It's a complicated story but you go from there.'

Writers don't usually have a say in where they interview celebrities. More often than not interviews with film and TV stars take place in anonymous hotel rooms with an endless stream of journalists filing in, one after the other, for an audience with the big name.

Better than hotels

But Brockes says that interviews come to life if you can talk to celebrities in a different setting. When she interviewed Liza Minnelli, for instance, she flew to Florida to watch her in concert, spoke to her backstage and then met her for lunch in New York. The interview was interrupted halfway through by a fire alarm and Brockes and Minnelli ended up walking together to another restaurant.

'You feel grateful for anything which puts the person you are interviewing in a context other than a bland hotel room,' says Brockes. 'Liza Minnelli and I went outside and sat on the steps and she started smoking. She didn't have to look me in the eye and she just suddenly started talking like a normal person.

'We often ask PRs to give us travelling time with a celebrity. I interviewed Richard Attenborough at his house and then, to get an extra 20 minutes, went with him in his car to Heathrow Airport. Just seeing the way he interacted with his driver, who'd been with him for 30 years, gave me more of a sense of the real person. He relaxed and was very jolly and funny.'

Some writers prefer to do interviews over lunch – but Brockes isn't one of them. 'When I do an interview over lunch I enjoy myself too much and you're not there to enjoy it. I think it's a bad idea to have a glass of wine, too, because you need to be really sharp and keep your wits about you.'

She admits though that interviewing involves a bit of luck, too, and very often a chance remark can send an interviewee in a direction she might not have thought of. 'The best example I've had is with Gwyneth Paltrow, who is really difficult to interview. I completely ran out of questions and in desperation asked her if she found that people drink more in Britain than in America. She suddenly started on this weird condemnation of women who drink, which was quite revealing.'

What not to do

Beforehand, during the interview Brockes keeps eye contact with the person she is talking to and doesn't look down at her notes. 'It really helps if they feel they are engaging with a human being who is responding to what they are saying and allowing them – to a certain extent – to dictate the interview as much as you are. All the stars I talk to about this say the thing that really kills them is when someone comes in with their 10 questions and nothing can divert them.'

One of Brockes's worst-ever interviews was with Australian film star Toni Collette, who, she says, was 'totally monosyllabic and didn't honour the transactional nature of these encounters'. Her favourites include the late novelist Muriel Spark, 'because she spoke in complete sentences and was brilliantly funny', actress Jeanne Moreau, 'for being very honest and French and scornful of the world', and former US secretary of state Madeleine Albright, who was 'brilliant and lovely and wanted to talk about how she couldn't get a date'.

So far Brockes hasn't had any recording disasters – she always uses a recorder and a notebook for interviews – but admits that most journalist friends she knows have. The only thing to do in those circumstances, she says, is to come clean, ring the interviewee up and ask for a few extra minutes on the phone. When she gets back to the office she immediately uploads her interview onto her computer – 'so much easier than having tapes jamming up your office' – and then transcribes it herself.

During the course of her career Brockes has interviewed hundreds of people all over the world and admits it's possible to get 'interviewed-out' if you do too many in a short space of time. But on the whole, she says, interviewing is 'absolutely brilliant. It is the most extraordinary privilege to parachute in, go straight to what you think is the most interesting part of someone's life and be able to ask the most impertinent questions they may ever have been asked.'

CASE STUDY 5 – ANDREW DUNCAN

Andrew Duncan's *Radio Times* interviews make national headlines. That alone would mark him out as exceptional. He's a talented tactician and joker, supremely and rightly confident in his talent.

He does not belong to that wearisome group of egomaniac journalists who appear to interview by looking in a mirror. He interviews celebrities, concentrating on them. He doesn't efface himself – a flavour of the man is there in his copy – but the 'I' count in his interviews is minimal. All this, plus an elegant, ironic style.

So why is he so good? Because he's a sympathetic listener, he says. If only it were that simple. Because he genuinely finds people interesting, he adds. A lot of us do, yet . . . Because he once sold encyclopaedias on commission in Toronto – yes, most certainly – also because he's disarming and assured at the same time. He gets seasoned, suspicious interviewees to drop their defences and he's always in control, though not all his interviewees realise it.

First, a warning for novice interviewers. Andrew Duncan is a very experienced journalist. He's perfected his interviewing technique after years of practice. He's generous, almost profligate, in talking about his approach to interviewing.

Here's a glimpse of his interview with Prince Edward. A PR was in attendance, as is always the case with royalty. Duncan describes her as 'some young girl from a TV station'. He silenced her by warning: 'If you say one word I'll get up and walk out and put that in the article.'

Talking to Prince Edward about the monarchy and Britain, he said:

> 'We're told there is a rigid class system, but it's a load of codswallop. I don't believe there's a class system, do you?'
>
> 'You're quite right,' said Prince Edward. 'There is no class system.'

Headlines, headlines, headlines. Sometimes people have to be drawn into admitting what they really think, he says. The skill here lies in the question and how it's phrased.

The same huge publicity surge followed Duncan's interview with Hugh Laurie, who told Duncan that, since he had started starring in *House* in the United States, he hadn't been offered any work in Britain. 'The door slammed behind me, and that's it. There's a notion that I've sold out,' he said.

The 'slammed door' quote was picked up around the world and Laurie contested its accuracy, demanding an apology, which he didn't get. Why? Because Duncan had recorded the interview, of course.

One last example of news-making interviews. With Mrs Thatcher after she had resigned, he used an approach that was shrewd, savvy but risky. Duncan asked for and was given an hour.

> I was told I couldn't discuss her time in power or her book, bought by the *Sunday Times*. So what on earth was the point of going to see her?
>
> I said: 'How nice to see you again. How's everything?' We chatted, and after about 10 minutes I said: 'That's it.' I started to pack up and prepare to leave, and naturally Mrs Thatcher was surprised. 'Well,' I said, 'I'm really sorry about this but I can't ask you about your time in office and I can't ask you about the book and the only questions I've got are rude ones.'
>
> 'Oh,' she said. 'We *love* rude questions.'
>
> 'Really?' I said. 'Why do you drink so much whisky?'
>
> 'What do you mean?'
>
> I said, 'Alan Clark's diaries, page 67.'

And away they went. Her sidekick began to look nervous, Duncan says, but the interview flowed on. He questioned her about relations with her son Mark and then the fact that there was no mention of her mother in her *Who's Who* entry. Duncan recalls: 'I'd taken the precaution of looking in *Who's Who*, then remembered my edition was two years old. When she queried it, I said: "I looked it up this morning." To which she replied: "Oh, then we must do something about that." ' Duncan put it in the *Radio Times* interview and the quote made headlines in every national UK paper. Not only then, he adds, but also on the anniversary, when she still had not put her mother into *Who's Who*.

So the lesson here is clear. He understood his quarry:

> Mrs Thatcher had an hour set aside. She programmed herself totally. An hour for this, an hour for that. When it looked as though the interview might end after 10 minutes, she had a three-quarter-hour yawning gap with nothing to do, so she had to continue and she did. It was a trap. I thought the odds were in my favour but of course she could have said, 'Thank you very much. That's fine.'

It's well known that politicians faced with a statement which they think may be based on rumour or guesswork demand substantiation.

> 'People say you . . .'
>
> 'Exactly who says so?'

Certainly the information about Mrs Thatcher drinking whisky came from Alan Clark's diaries and sounded good and convincing, whether Duncan quoted the right page or not.

Preparation

Having glimpsed Duncan's style, let's go sequentially through his interviewing process, starting with setting up the interview. This is normally arranged by *Radio Times*. He always asks for an hour alone with the interviewee. PRs are forbidden, unless the circumstances are exceptional (royals, for instance).

And the location? For him, a good lunch in a good restaurant, which helps his interviewees relax. New York, LA, Rome, Paris, all suit him well. He always orders champagne, because it makes the occasion festive, he says. Not surprisingly, he avoids the BBC canteen and dislikes interviewing on set.

Research? 'I do a huge amount. I get all the cuttings.' They're couriered or emailed to him. He normally has a list of 60 or so questions in his head and says he usually gets through 40 to 60 of them. 'I get really cross if I haven't done them in an hour.' He makes it his business to discover some recondite piece of information that they wouldn't expect him to know. 'I bring this in at a very early stage. They say: "How do you know that?" ' This signals to them not to try any wool-pulling. You will always get programmed answers at the start, he says, but he tries to get rid of them in the first few minutes.

'Far too many celebrities have contempt for journalists,' says Duncan, 'and that's quite disturbing, although I think they're right. So many journalists don't do their homework or have the courtesy to know what the guy they're interviewing has done.'

His preparation does not include changing his clothes to match his interviewee's.

> My absolute fundamental is always wear a suit. I thought with Noel Gallagher, if I dress down it will look as if I'm trying too hard, like parents of teenagers trying to be teenagers. But I realised I had to explain, so I said: 'I'm very sorry but I'm going to see the Inland Revenue.' 'I thought you *were* the Inland Revenue, he said.

In the south of France, though, he did wear shorts when interviewing Robbie Williams.

If he isn't granted an hour for the interview he compensates by putting in a huge amount of extra research. With Johnny Depp, for example, the time offered was so limited that Duncan opted for three more days' research, including attending all the 'group' interviews where any number of journalists have a limited time to ask their questions. Duncan asked no questions – of course – but watched Depp's body language and listened to all his replies for hints or clues of valuable lines to pursue during his interview.

A sympathetic listener

Duncan uses a digital, state-of-the-art recorder, setting it up very matter-of-factly on the table. With a much-interviewed celebrity he may begin with a cheerful disclaimer. 'Let's start by agreeing that everything that's been printed about you is rubbish and this'll probably be more lies, so let's just have a nice lunch.' This gets them on your side, he says.

He never appears – please note the word *appears* – to take the interview too seriously. Sometimes he says: 'Don't worry about a thing. I've written it already, and this is just a performance.' He's a very sympathetic listener, and laughs and smiles a lot. 'I want people to think of me as a mate, someone who doesn't give a stuff, only asking these questions because he can't think of anything else.'

He keeps an unobtrusive eye on the recorder and has only once had it fail. This was when he was interviewing Michael Palin.

> He spoke very movingly for the first time about his sister's suicide. Fantastic, and I thought: 'God, you're clever, Andrew.' I kept looking at my recorder, checking it.
>
> I got back and was going to transcribe it and it was blank. What I'd done, I think, was put the microphone into the earpiece, so it still showed it was playing. In a total panic I phoned the manufacturers. Is there any way, however much it costs, to retrieve it? They said no.

He was too ashamed to tell Palin the truth at the time, though he told him later, so he concocted some story about the recorder being stolen. They repeated the interview but, as to be expected, it wasn't so good. The upshot, says Duncan, is that now he's terrified and checks all the time, carrying a pair of earphones with him.

Never disagree

So where does selling encyclopaedias in Toronto come in? Duncan says:

> The best training. It's sheer hell. You're dropped off in the morning in some small town or village and left there. What you learn is that you never, ever, disagree with anyone. If they say it's too expensive you say: 'Absolutely. I quite agree.'

He's very good at reading people, so if he knows there's a subject they don't want to talk about, he'll adopt one of several approaches depending on their character. Perhaps he'll avoid all mention, approaching the dangerous subject but veering off at the last moment. Sometimes he'll make a contract covering what they'll talk about.

Duncan used this second technique on Harrison Ford, and included it in his intro:

> Here is the agreement – I promise not to mention the C word [carpenter] to him if he tries not to be the boring 'terrible interviewee' he claims to be.
>
> He smiles. 'I'm quite good really, but on my terms – that we discuss the work, and you ask fascinating questions.'

In the end, of course, they got round to the C word.

Duncan hates agents who try to establish what subjects can and can't be included. He says he'll ask what he likes and the subject is quite entitled to tell him to mind his own business. Sometimes this backfires. Actress Robin Givens, formerly married to boxer Mike Tyson, said she wouldn't answer questions about Tyson. 'Is it true that he beat you?' Duncan asked. Givens turned off her own recorder and walked out.

Robert Redford

Duncan hates news management with the fierceness of a journalist who has seen the noose tighten. Marvel at this intro:

> The second floor of the exclusive Crillon Hotel in Paris is agog with self-importance. Thigh-booted girls, impossibly tall and gloatingly gorgeous, do important things with mobile telephones; haughty, frock-coated waiters glide by with trays of tea; a film crew, latched electronically together, perspires on the stairs; a trio of middle-aged women smoke furiously in a state of post-interview *tristesse*; a girl sits at a desk cluttered with lists, name tags and folders of information; another clicks a button on her stopwatch, groans and ushers a group into the presence of the 'talent'. I flick through instructions of where his photographs must be retouched . . . 'the wrinkled area between his lower lip and chin', 'the veins on his nose', 'the area around the neck and throat', 'soften the forehead lines'.

Oh artifice, thy name is a superstar interview. There are far fewer fol-de-rols in meeting a president, a prime minister, a royal. Yet such is Robert Redford's practised charm and, it seems, genuine modesty, that all frustrations disappear on meeting.

Duncan remembers how, during the interview, he'd ask Redford a question and . . .

> He'd answer with a quote I'd read in the *New York Times* about a totally different question. Like: 'I was in Paris in the early days and before I answer this question I just want to tell you how much I love Paris.' I said: 'I've read this in connection with another question. What I asked you was . . .'

The ploy Duncan finds most effective for many celebrities, particularly those who have got to hide their mixed-up backgrounds, is what he calls 'the Arthur Miller quote'. It still works, he says, even though Miller died in 2005 – and it obviously can be adapted to someone more up to date.

> It goes this way: you say something along the following lines: 'I was talking to Arthur Miller some time back and he said that to be really creative you have to have a fairly dysfunctional background. That really helps. Do you think that's true?'
>
> They've heard of Arthur Miller and say, 'Oh my God, yes.'

Duncan admits to a lot of name-dropping and says sometimes he feels nauseated when he listens to the recorder. 'I'm hideously creepy.'

He immerses himself in the cuttings but scorns using other people's material. 'It's got to be fresh. It can't be a cuttings job.' That's why he gets nervous before his interviews. He has to get all his material then and there.

Elton John

Duncan says the only time he ever used a cuttings quote was with Elton John, because he didn't have the time to prepare properly for the interview, thinking Elton would cancel on him. He acknowledges that he had been rather prejudiced against 'the lachrymose pudding'.

Knowing that Elton admired Versace, he arrived for the interview wearing a Versace tie and managed to let one of Elton's CDs fall out of the bag he was carrying. He didn't expect to like Elton, but he did. They both have houses in the south of France, so common ground was established fairly quickly, and it moved the interview onto a totally different level. 'He was brilliant. I liked him, I really liked him.'

Duncan's least favourite but curiously most quote-worthy interviewees are sports people, tennis players in particular, but he enjoys politicians because they're used to being asked questions – though not the sort he asks. 'It's only in this job that you talk to people about subjects so intimate that your parents or your best friend wouldn't discuss them with you. You get to ask questions which are terribly personal, cheeky and offensive.'

Such questions provoke a response from most people, but politicians are tougher meat. The best thing for them, says Duncan, is to make them feel sorry for you. 'If you can pretend complete ignorance they become terribly pompous and give away a side of themselves not always seen.' An important caveat here: this approach may work in political celebrity interviews but it is not for straightforward political interviews.

Duncan concludes: 'You have to be in control. Otherwise it's no good.

'Interviewing is a craft,' he says, 'an act – liking people and not appearing to take it too seriously. If you're really interested it comes across.'

CASE STUDY 6 – LYNDA LEE-POTTER

As well as being a great columnist, earning her the title 'First Lady of Fleet Street', Lynda Lee-Potter was a gifted feature writer and an outstanding interviewer. She is greatly missed, but her advice – originally given in the first edition of this book – lives on.

She trained as an actress – appearing on the West End stage before she married – which gave her an acute ear for dialogue. She could read unattributed quotes and know who said them, read so-called quotes from people she'd interviewed and know they were not the interviewee's words. More than that, she was intuitive, able to stand between two people at a party and know that they were having an affair.

The key to interviewing, she said, is to concentrate totally.

> When I'm interviewing, nothing else will get in the way. People talk about 'Doctor Theatre' – actors who will go on stage with a broken leg. Certainly when interviewing if you've got flu or pneumonia, it goes completely. You concentrate so

totally that you lose yourself and you lose your aches and pains. Wonderful therapy, because for that time nothing intrudes.

My way is to speak as little as possible and keep my questions incredibly simple and brief. The best interview is when you get that invisible cord between the two of you. You want to make the person you are talking to feel fascinating and the object of your whole being, which indeed they are.

Interviewing is a job you never, ever crack.

In the shadows

Lee-Potter almost always wore black. 'It happens subconsciously actually. You're not the star. And it works. I've often seen people several times over the years and they very rarely remember me.' This is a recognised sign of a great interviewer, though not recognised enough by beginners and the bombastic. Lee-Potter interviewed celebrities but shunned being a 'celebrity interviewer'. 'I'm in the shadows,' she said. 'That's the way I prefer it.'

Preparation

She did as much preparation as possible – read all the cuttings, biogs, found out as much as possible about the person she was to interview. 'There's nothing worse than going to see somebody and asking an incredibly naff question about something you should know.'

In an ideal world she'd always want at least two hours for the interview at the interviewee's house. Because she believed it's unforgivable to arrive late, she was always there hours early. She hadn't the nerve to ring the doorbell two hours early so parked the car in a lay-by. She used the time rereading her research and looking over her questions so she could go in prepared. 'If you arrive late and flustered and forget the questions you want to ask, the first half hour will be wasted. There's no excuse for being late. You must allow time for things to go wrong.'

She said she was always terrified beforehand. 'My tummy turns over. I'm always anxious. Always. Always.' She might ring the bell half an hour before the agreed time. 'I always say: "I'm sorry I'm too early. Shall I go away?" Sometimes they'll say "Yes", sometimes "Come in".'

She starts the interview almost straightaway, having sussed out the room.

> When you walk in it's very important to case the joint and know where you're going to sit and where they're going to sit. If they show you into the drawing room and then go out, that's marvellous. If we're meeting in a restaurant, I have been known to move three times before the interviewee arrives. The killer situation is to be sitting opposite at a table or desk. It makes people rigid.

She would set up two recorders, usually one either side of the table, 'because you never know if anything will go wrong', and then start. Her method, she said was to make people feel relaxed, warm, loved and at ease, beginning gently and concentrating on her interviewee completely.

Fresh questions

Unless you're interviewing someone who, once prompted, can go into a monologue, then you and your interviewee are dependent on the questions. She would arrive with a list of questions but by the end might not have asked them all. 'Listening is vital. They'll say something and you'll think, God, I must ask this . . . The more research you have done, the easier it is.'

Her questions were simple, brief and precise. 'If you ask fresh questions, you'll get a fresh interview. Don't ask hackneyed questions and you won't get hackneyed answers.'

That great interviewing gift – sensitivity – worked for her. 'You've got to have an antenna, an instinct,' she said. 'You can sense things. Suddenly a question will come from nowhere and you don't know why you've asked it.' She matched her interviewing technique to her interviewee.

> In a way it's like being a psychiatrist. You've got to find the right way to ask. We're all different with different people. With the Commons hooker Pamella Bordes I discovered the only way to get her to tell you anything was to be really quite aggressive. Someone being aggressive to me would shut me up.

Some interviewees asked, 'What's your angle?' She told them she hadn't got an angle.

> I just want to let them emerge as they are – boring, fascinating, tedious, witty or monsters – I mostly do it through quotes because I think people are revealed through what they say much more vividly than anything I might write. Everyone has a different way of writing. I rely on quotes tremendously.

Living dangerously

As an interviewer, Lee-Potter had no recourse to tricks or deception, but she admitted that wine helped. It established a camaraderie, she said. Though she admitted to being 'slightly in charge', she didn't believe in being too controlling: 'I like to let the conversation gather its own momentum and sometimes let them take control. I'm all for "Let's live dangerously and see what happens".'

When things go wrong

'People's faces when they're being interviewed are incredibly revealing. You can see in their eyes when something goes wrong,' Lee-Potter said. 'You can see if they're cross or rattled. Sometimes, if they're rattled, it's important to press on. Again, it's an instinct to know when you have to withdraw instantly and change tack.'

There is a moment, she said, when they suddenly get bored. 'You can see it in their eyes and know they'll start repeating themselves. It's very important you spot that.' However, she rarely left until she was asked to. 'I stay to the bitter end. I can't think off-hand of any interview where I've gone of my own volition.'

When it comes to writing the interview up, quoting accurately was her passion.

> An approximation of what they say is not good enough. Everybody has an idiosyncratic way of talking and to get the meaning over without actually using the way they use words isn't good enough.
>
> Sometimes I'll read interviews with people I've interviewed and I'll know there's no way they'd ever have said that. They wouldn't use those words. They might express that meaning

but not speak in that way. If you get what they say right, they're often happy with the interview. They're less likely to be happy if you get it wrong.

Lee-Potter's list of what not to do:

- Don't take your eyes off your interviewee.
- Don't think you have to be bold and daring and prove how clever you are by asking questions early on about subjects you've been warned against. Ask gently but not until the end of the interview
- Don't interrupt people, particularly famous actors, in the middle of anecdotes, even if you've read the story in the cuttings several times. Fatal. You have got to let them tell it and then not use it.
- If someone says 'This is off the record', *never* try to double-cross them – because you only double-cross people once. They know, they remember, they tell their friends.

CASE STUDY 7 – JAN MASTERS TALKS TO AMBER TOKELEY

She's shared a laugh with Renée Zellweger, gone hiking with Heather Graham and received a charming but unnecessary apology from Will Smith. Interviewing celebrities is 'not nearly as scary as you might think', says Jan Masters, who has written for a wide range of titles including *Elle*, *Radio Times* and *InStyle*.

Although celebrity interviews are normally organised by the commissioning magazine, the journalist may be required to sign an agreement, such as one-off use. Masters warns: 'Be aware of what you've signed.' You don't want to find yourself in hot water trying to reuse information elsewhere at some future date.

Movie databases

There are various specialist research tools including the internet movie database, IMDb (www.imdb.com), which lists people's filmographies, biographies, what they're working on next, and so on. It's also worth checking out their personal website and subscribing to online reference sources such as HighBeam (www.highbeam.com), and asking the commissioning magazine if they will do a cuts run (a special search on magazines and newspapers). It's also easy to do archive searches of individual publications.

Although Masters always prepares questions, she says: 'Be ready to deviate at any moment.' Time can also be an issue, especially if the celebrity has a busy schedule and has to wind up early, so be aware of it: 'Look at the time ticking on your recording equipment because if you glance down at that it seems as though you are just checking your recording equipment.'

Masters plays safe by running two digital recorders at an interview, and checks that the batteries are fresh. She recommends loading the recording onto your computer as soon as possible so that it's on a hard drive, and then backing it up.

'It's also good to really understand your recording equipment,' she says. 'If it's new, really play around with it first and see how it works. Otherwise, you could delete something without meaning to.'

Before the interview, ensure that both the publicist and the magazine have your contact numbers, because interviews are often delayed. 'Be prepared to wait,' says Masters. 'Celebrities' schedules often are ludicrously tight and things change all the time.'

That said, some stars do their best to be punctual. Masters cites Hollywood superstar Will Smith. 'His publicist came down to me in the hotel and said: "He apologises but he is going to be 10 minutes late." And I thought "what a gentleman!" because for five or 10 minutes you wouldn't even bother. That was so ultra-professional.'

The interview

Smile, shake their hand if it looks like they are about to shake yours. And be yourself. 'I was always surprised at how relaxed it was,' says Masters, who prefers to start with some small talk.

'If I've had a terrible journey, I might say: "Oh, I'm so glad I'm here, I thought I wasn't going to make it in time." If they have done a lot of interviews that day, I'll say something like "Are you really bored?" or "You must be tired". It shows you are human rather than just going in and saying "Right, I've got these questions . . . ".'

She 'involves' them in setting up her equipment, which also helps get things on a normal, friendly footing: 'I always say "Ooh, I'm just double-checking the recorder is on as I don't want a disaster".' If it is noisy she will ask the celebrity if she can set the recorder extra-close to them, as she did with Calista Flockhart in a busy diner. Sometimes an interview will take place over a meal. 'I always order something that only requires a fork and that's soft, so I go for risotto or fishcake,' says Masters – less risk of embarrassing yourself, that way.

Occasionally, you might end up interviewing a celebrity in an unconventional situation. This makes for good copy so embrace it, but be upfront about handling technical problems – it's in their interest to work with you. Masters recalls having to interview the American actress Heather Graham while hiking around the Hollywood Hills. 'It was a lovely day and she said "wouldn't it be nice to go for a walk?" ' Apart from the challenge of keeping up with her, Masters's main concern was recording clarity due to wind noise. 'I just said "that's fine, if you don't mind me thrusting this recorder your way".'

Press junkets are another challenge, since you will be just one of many journalists the celebrity will be talking to that day. 'The best thing is to start with a really quirky question that's going to make them laugh and refresh their brain a bit,' says Masters. 'Think of something unexpected that isn't necessarily about the film they are publicising.'

If a subject is off-limits, the publicist will brief you beforehand, and Masters believes it is important to respect that. However, if she needs to ask a sensitive question she is straightforward: 'I'll say "Here I am, doing my job and asking this slightly awkward question but feel free to tell me to shut up". And they generally say "Well . . . I don't like to talk about it but I *will* say . . .".'

The most revealing information often emerges not from 'must-know' facts but from simple conversation: 'It might be that I say, "Ooh my mum always says that," and they say "my mother always says . . ." You are much more likely to get an interesting answer that way than by simply asking, "What does your mother tell you?" '

Always keep in mind lead times, which may be several months away, because they can drastically impact on the relevance of your questions

– for example, the celebrity who has just got engaged could be married by publication date.

Because Masters records her interviews, she takes very few notes. 'I prefer to look in their eyes and chat with them properly. The scribbling tends to be about background colour.' That's what brings an interview to life, so take note of everything going on around you. 'Often, when interviewing, something will happen and I will think "that's my opener". It may be a fan asking for their autograph or – worst case scenario – you walk in and trip over. Then I would start: "I met at blah-blah's feet . . ." '

If you are doing a phone interview (called 'phoners'), get the interviewee to describe where they are and what they are doing so you can still weave colour into the story.

As with all types of interviews, keep an eye on the time, and know when to start winding up – try not to put the onus on them. 'I often say "I'm aware of your time, and you've got to go. Can I just squeeze in a word or two about . . . ?" '

The A-listers are old hands at the publicity game and are usually easy to talk to, says Masters. So enjoy the interview – it's the best part. And remember – if you're eating and interviewing, *don't* order the lobster!

11 Challenging interviewees

Reluctant interviewees, inexperienced interviewees, business people, vulnerable people, children and the bereaved ('death knocks' and 'fatals' in newspaper jargon) all require special handling, as do interviews where PRs sit in on the interview, and what's called 'two-handers', where it's the interviewers who double up.

Reluctant interviewees

You have maybe two seconds before they slam the door on you. What can you do? Try stepping back. This is unexpected and, in a strange way, magnetic. As you step back they seem drawn forward.

If they don't shout at you to get off their property or slam the door in your face at this point, they'll probably agree to talk eventually if you're subtle. Say who you are and what you are doing, then there can be no mistake about why you are there, says experienced doorstepper Mike Biggs, formerly with Brennan's news agency at Heathrow.

Never park directly outside the house and certainly don't adopt an aggressive or eager tone of voice. The key is to make it clear that there's a need for their side of the story and you're offering them that opportunity. You say something like:

> 'People keep making these allegations and for your own protection you have to put your point of view.'
>
> 'How do you answer what . . . is saying?'
>
> 'It looks bad if you don't comment. We'd like to print your side of the story.'

Don't take offence, however much they swear at you or whatever insults they pour on you or your paper. Stay cool and calm and keep repeating that what's being said about them needs to be answered and they are the ones best placed to do that.

Listen and sympathise

You can defuse their fury by listening. You don't have to agree with them in their rant – though that is often a great way to deflect anger – but you can soothe using sympathy.

> 'Lies, lies! – All bloody lies – ruining my life!'
> 'I can see that it must be a terrible worry for you and the family.'
> 'How would you like it if the bloody bitch said that about you?'
> 'I'd hate it – and I'd want to defend myself . . .'
> 'Why should I talk to you? You printed those vile allegations.'
> 'We can't print what we don't know. If what . . . says is false, tell me what really happened.'

Make it plain that talking to you will benefit them. You're there to help them clear their name. Never say any of the following:

> 'Come off it!'
>
> 'How could you?'
>
> 'That was stupid.'
>
> 'You didn't, surely?'

When to use your notebook

Keep your notebook in your pocket at first. The time to bring it out is after they've relaxed and invited you in, or when they've said something telling or incriminating that requires further comment.

> 'You said . . .'

Alternatively, use a digital recorder or go straight back to the car and write down everything you can remember, timed and dated in your notebook (see page 108).

If you suspect the interview is going to be tricky and/or dangerous, then take someone along as a witness, but warn them *not* to join in the questioning. You may be picking a delicate path that leads gently to a crucial question. The interviewee may hesitate, poised on the brink of a revealing answer, when the idiot with you, unused to pauses and interviewing techniques, jumps in with a question that destroys your whole carefully constructed sequence.

Keep on asking the question you want answered. Rephrase it, walk round it, approach it from a variety of ways. Get to the nitty-gritty by persistence – and remember you are there for the readers, asking the questions they'd like answered.

Inexperienced interviewees

They may be wary or trusting, indiscreet or guarded, but all first-time interviewees are unused to dealing with the press, so don't foul it up for those who follow. An ordinary person interviewed just once in a lifetime by a journalist probably tells 30 other people about the experience; any poor practice just kicks us all further down the list of the trustworthy – and we're already rated on a par with estate agents.

Inexperienced interviewees usually need the least cajoling of any to take part. But you must handle them with care. Make sure they give you clear directions to your arranged meeting place: for example, get the actual names of the roads rather than 'second on the left after the bridge', and repeat them back at least once. A map or Sat would be so much better. Always ask for their mobile number, or check where they will be immediately before the planned interview, just in case you are delayed or have to cancel. Also, always ask for more time than usual, since the preliminaries often take up 10 to 15 minutes.

It's important when fixing the interview to give them a good but not too detailed idea of what you want to talk about. Excess information often results in over-rehearsed answers, which lack vitality.

Easy does it

As ever, try to arrive in good time, although this is one occasion where your novelty value means that short delays will be forgiven. Prepare to be looked over very thoroughly and to answer an assortment of questions about the publication, your job, other interviews you've done. Be human and agreeable. Smile. This is an occasion where being brisk and business-like is a mistake, so don't be in a hurry.

Wipe your feet carefully and shed any wet weather gear in the porch. Don't sit down until asked to do so and if you're offered tea or coffee, accept. Refusing appears rude and gets things off to a bad start. It also gives the interviewee a chance to exit to the kitchen and update any family or friends, should they be there, about you. You'll be forgiven at the end if you haven't finished your drink – they will think it's because you found the interview so riveting.

Take your time to greet everyone in the room, including the cat or dog. Don't rush the preliminaries but, when they're over, offer your interviewee a copy of the publication if appropriate, your card, and take out your notebook and/or recorder. Don't start though until your interviewee is settled.

Most inexperienced interviewees will be curious rather than apprehensive and will be looking forward to the interview, so make it a pleasant experience. Explain again what you're after so they can collect their thoughts. If they appear nervous, then proceed calmly and gently. Verbal reassurance is often counter-productive, rather like saying to a child going to the dentist for the first time, 'Don't worry – it won't hurt!'

Start with a question on a safe subject that you know they can answer with ease. Get them relaxed and talking before you approach any difficult or tricky areas. Depending on the subject of the interview, having more than one person in the room can either help or hinder. If the interview is about some achievement or event, then input from others with anecdotes and colourful details can be very valuable.

If it's about relationships and/or traumas, then you must accept that sometimes what's said will be coloured by who else is in the room and may be said for their benefit rather than yours. This is tricky, and devising ways to get an interviewee on their own can be difficult. Try sending other people out to get more tea, locate photographs etc. – but it doesn't always work.

Fair warning

With inexperienced interviewees, you will almost always find yourself in complete control. It's a rare first-time interviewee who has worked out an agenda and answers accordingly. Most will do their best to be helpful and answer your questions fully, so these must be devised to bring out the story you're after. You'll find silence works wonderfully well here – long pauses usually prompt an inexperienced interviewee to rush to fill the gap, which often reveals useful or unexpected information.

Your interviewee may also be vulnerable because of lack of experience, and you may have to decide whether to warn them not to be indiscreet. If you're told 'We bought this old picture for just £15 because we wanted the frame, and then discovered it was an early Lord Leighton. We sold it for £280,000', do you check with them whether they have declared capital gains tax, and warn them that the Inland Revenue reads papers and magazines for just this sort of information?

If, in the course of recounting how they have triumphed over some tragedy, they let slip just how much trouble they have encountered from thoughtless neighbours, do you suggest they consider how this will look in print? You may feel that such moral judgements are not part of the job, or you may believe that when people are vulnerable, showing consideration is part of responsible journalism. Over to you.

Either way, you need to realise that your attentive listening and encouraging comments may beguile them into saying much, much more than they intended. Using such techniques is fair game when people are in the public eye, or are nominated by their firms to talk to the press, but is it fair for the inexperienced? You decide.

Business people

The bigger the corporation, the more intensive and expensive the media training its executives will have received – almost certainly more than the journalists who interview them.

This is not only because time is money, although if a highly paid executive is going to give up an hour of his day to talk to a journalist there must be something in it for the corporation. It's also because any company listed on a stock exchange is supposed, in theory, to give important information to the exchange and its shareholders before telling anyone else.

From the company's viewpoint executives need to know they should avoid any public comment that might move the company's share price up or down. Ken Gooding, former specialist writer for the *Financial Times*, explains:

> Corporations have just as much at stake as senior politicians when their executives are interviewed. An ill-judged, off-the-cuff remark from a senior executive can damage a company, as Gerald Ratner, the boss of a popular jewellery chain, found when he jokingly described one of the products sold in his shops as 'crap'. He became a laughing stock and later was forced out of the company.

Company executives, Gooding says, also have more reason to be economical with the truth than politicians. 'When interviewing a business person you don't know well, it's best to ask yourself at frequent intervals, "Why is this lying bastard lying to me?"' But, he says, it's very important not to let these thoughts show. Most senior business people have large egos. 'Often that's what has driven them up the corporate ladder.' They're surrounded by staff who treat them deferentially – certainly not asking rude or mocking questions or making critical remarks.

It is possible, Gooding says, to ask difficult questions and still remain on friendly terms with your interviewee by making it clear the criticism has been levelled by someone else.

> You say, 'One of your competitors suggests that there have been problems with that particular model and it is difficult to control at high speeds. Is there any truth in that?', rather than, 'That model has a terrible reputation for swerving all over the place on motorways. What are you going to do about it?'

Given what's at stake, it's no wonder that business people are so highly trained. During practice interviews they learn how to take control, how to make the points they want to make no matter what they're asked, and how to deal with possible 'difficult' questions. (To see this in practice, watch a TV interview with politicians.)

It's also no wonder that PRs figure largely on corporate payrolls, or that smaller companies employ outside consultants. The aim is to exert as much control over the press as possible. PRs advise on which journalists and publications to talk to, a selection often based on which can be trusted to be accurate.

PRs usually brief executives about the journalist before the interview – not just their CV but also about recent work and whether the journalist is likely to be 'friendly' to the company. Big corporations will almost certainly ask any journalist requesting an interview to provide beforehand an indication of topics to be covered and some of the questions to be asked. The ostensible reason is that statistics etc. can be provided at the meeting. Really, though, says Gooding, it's because one of the first rules in business is that 'there should be no surprises'.

Importantly, this forces the journalist to research and think carefully about how the interview should be structured. Thorough research for business interviews is essential, Gooding says.

> The journalist needs to have a clear idea of what they want to achieve or the interviewee will set the agenda and take complete control. Read the cuttings, talk to competitors, prepare soft questions, not-so-soft questions and the approach you will use when asking the hard questions.

No need to waste time on preliminaries – a quick greeting and get down to business. You definitely need to know how long you have, as business interviews very rarely overrun.

Beware, Gooding says, of the PR who wishes to sit behind you (see also page 185). Be aware that any attempts to flatter you are designed to make you feel better disposed to the company and to take up your valuable time in an unproductive way. 'Why otherwise would a captain of industry ask a journalist who has probably never run a whelk stall for an opinion on how the company should operate?'

Few executives will talk freely to a journalist they neither know nor trust. One way to gain trust is to be flexible. Gooding suggests:

> Offer to go off the record at any time the interviewee wishes to. And, to emphasise your trustworthiness, ostentatiously switch off your recorder. You might even allow some second thoughts and when an executive says 'I think that should be off the record', go along with it. You can learn more and have a better understanding of the company's business that way.

Obviously, he says, executives very rarely go on the record when dishing the dirt on competitors. 'Often, if a journalist is to fully understand a complex situation, some confidential background has to be provided by an off-the-record briefing.'

It's comforting, he says, that although during the interview the corporation holds most of the cards, the journalist is in charge of the material. However, he believes specialists need to tread a careful line.

> You're not going to be very effective if you upset too many people in the industry so they talk to you only under sufferance. On the other hand, you don't want to be seen as an industry 'mouthpiece' and part of its PR efforts.

Only by doing the research, knowing as much as possible about the full picture, by being accurate and fair in your reporting and comments, can you achieve this. When you say you won't quote someone, you don't quote them. When you give undertakings, you stick to them.

Vulnerable people

At some time during their careers, many journalists have to interview vulnerable people: perhaps distraught middle-aged parents whose only daughter is in a coma after a hit-and-run accident; or a confused and frightened 70-year-old man whose hip has been broken in a mugging; or a young mother whose child has been abducted.

These interviews are often easier than the beginner expects. Provided you are sympathetic, take your time and listen, the story will usually pour out. In fact, in the immediate aftermath, people are often desperate to talk. What stops the flow is an interviewer's brisk or brusque efficiency in getting to the facts which implies a lack of empathy, coupled with a 'hurry-up-I'm-on-deadline' approach. Best to let them unload: try to guide them very gently and carefully so that you end up with the information you need.

The bereaved and injured are in shock, so talking about what's happened usually helps them, acting as some form of therapy. However, the emotionally vulnerable, such as a rape victim or someone with a particular disorder, are usually wary and very reluctant to relive painful events or talk about unusual behaviour that may be condemned or misunderstood by the majority. Interviewing them is much harder and requires delicacy.

It is a great help to be introduced to them by someone they have faith in – their counsellor, therapist or social worker – and it's essential before you meet them to put yourself, as much as possible, into their shoes.

How would you feel if at 82 your beloved wife of 60 years developed Alzheimer's and you were too frail to cope with 24-hour care? How would you feel if you discovered your son was abusing other children at his school? How would you react if your husband left you for another man?

It's well worth checking out the relevant charity organisation websites from bereavement to specific disorders and diseases; they often provide useful guidelines to understanding the problem and communicating effectively with the person affected.

When interviewing vulnerable people, reporters may have to be creative in working out how to achieve the most effective result and interview at a distance. A journalist working for the in-house magazine of an international organisation recalls having to write a case study for her company's work programme for vulnerable people. The employee concerned had Down syndrome and worked in another part of the country, and a face-to-face interview was not an option. However, a telephone interview seemed inappropriate, given its potential for creating unnecessary stress and confusion for the vulnerable interviewee.

So the journalist discussed it with the employee's line manager, offering a range of options which she then put to the employee with Down syndrome. He decided he would be most comfortable being emailed written questions which he could then go through with his manager, who transcribed his answers and returned them to the journalist.

Gaining trust

Slowly and very gently is the way to approach vulnerable people. You have to gain their trust if they're to tell you their story. This takes time. Freelance Joy Melville, who has specialised in such interviews, says you must never rush.

It's crucial, she says, to accept any offer of tea they make. She instances just one exception which occurred when she interviewed a woman who was obsessive about dirt and germs.

> I had permission from her therapist to see her and when I got there she had put sheets all the way down the hall, right through the sitting room and all over the chair where I was going to sit.

> The therapist had warned me that whatever I did, not to go to the loo, because it would have taken her a day to ensure it was properly clean.
>
> 'But I said yes to tea, thinking it would put her at her ease. She watched me intently while I drank the tea and when I finished she leapt up and I think she spent 25 minutes in the kitchen scouring the cup and saucer.

Vulnerable interviewees are particularly suspicious and need to be convinced that you understand and approve of what they're revealing about themselves. 'They're picking up signs all the time,' Melville says. 'I often say, "Oh yes, I do agree, because the same has happened to me." If they feel you aren't shocked, they're encouraged to say "And there's another thing . . ."'

Not everyone will like the idea, but in her experience it often helps, she says, to put yourself down deliberately; for instance, if you are talking about disastrous relationships, you might say, 'Oh yes, every single man/woman I've ever known has eventually dumped me.' This may or may not be true, she says, but you're trying not to upstage them. 'You're saying they're not the only person who's experienced this, the only person who's mucked it up. They mustn't think that everyone else copes better than they do.'

Always be sympathetic

Encapsulated advice for interviewers is usually 'Be sceptical, not adversarial'. Encapsulated advice when interviewing the emotionally vulnerable is '*Never* be anything other than sympathetic'.

Melville instances agoraphobics, men and women who have a fear of leaving, or going any distance from, their home.

> Agoraphobics never starve. There's always a partner, a neighbour, who does the shopping. If the partner dies or the neighbour moves away, the agoraphobic will venture out a short distance to find someone else – but if you even imply they could go outside, they say, 'You don't understand, do you? You just don't understand how I feel. Have you ever had a phobia yourself?' And they work themselves up into an absolute anger and then they can say: 'It's useless. Why don't you go?'

Instead of challenging an agoraphobic, you get results by being sympathetic and interested, Melville says, and by asking oblique questions. 'How do the children get to school? Who takes them?' Your face, she says, often becomes 'a mask of sympathy'.

No laughing matter

Never laughing is just as important as never passing negative judgements on what a vulnerable person tells you. Melville remembers a woman who was arachnophobic – terrified of spiders.

> She told me, 'I saw this spider and I threw a telephone directory at it and it moved four inches to the left and defied me!' It was very hard not to say, 'Did it have a gun?' as opposed to 'How awful', but I don't like spiders so I was sympathetic. It's often very hard not to laugh but you must never, ever.
>
> You put your hand over your mouth and pull the skin of your cheekbones back, all the time looking down at your notebook, then no one can see your eyes laughing.

Or else you can turn an incipient laugh into a cough or, as a last resort, bite the inside of your cheeks – then it's impossible to laugh.

Melville uses shorthand and believes that the fact she is not staring intently at people but looking down at her notebook and then glancing up to smile at appropriate moments often encourages confidences. 'A chiropodist once told me he heard the most amazing things from people *because* he had his back to them, working on their feet.' This is not accepted wisdom in journalism, which sets great store by eye contact, but consider: the same principle is employed by the priest in the confessional, or by the psychiatrist sitting out of sight of the patient on the couch.

Interviewing people with mental health problems can be traumatic for the interviewer. Here, the focus should be on your safety: never go alone to a meeting without taking your mobile phone. Often it can be far better to interview them in an appropriate public place, such as a day centre, with professional back-up – though not applicable for agoraphobics, naturally. Or consider providing written questions for them to look at first, or perhaps discuss with their psychiatrist if that makes them feel more comfortable.

Melville once went to interview a schizophrenic young woman of about 18.

> Her mother opened the door, looking very old and tired with the trauma she was going through with her daughter. The daughter was in a nest of blankets and she leapt up, looked at me and said 'Right after you phoned I decided to shave my head' – and she had.
>
> This was a very difficult interview because at the same time she was talking to me she was also having a conversation with King Tutankhamun. She'd say something to me and then look over her shoulder and say 'I don't see why I should die young just because you died young. Just because you died young, doesn't mean I've got to' – and then she'd go on talking to me.
>
> At one point, she suddenly scribbled something down on a piece of paper, scrunched it up, threw it down and ran out of the room. Of course in true journalistic style I leapt for the wastepaper basket. She'd written: 'I know where I'm going but I don't want to go.'
>
> It was really very, very sad. Afterwards I felt I had to go and talk to her mother and say thank you, because the mother never got out of the house, had this daughter rampaging round, sometimes running out of the house at 2 o'clock in the morning.

The long goodbye

Just as it takes longer to start an interview with a vulnerable person, testing the emotional temperature, so it also takes much longer to say goodbye. The interview may be over but you shouldn't leave until you're sure your interviewee is contented. Melville says:

> Addicts, or people who are suffering from depression, are often extremely vulnerable. After you've talked to them for a while you may know you have got enough for the article, but it's at that point they have decided you are sympathetic and understanding.
>
> If you leave that house within a couple of hours you are very lucky. They absolutely offload everything on to you. In effect you

are the stranger on the train to whom they can tell all, not the judgemental friend or relation who said 'I told you that would happen!'

You may be exhausted but you feel they have allowed you into their home and that you can't just walk into their lives, interview them, then say 'Thank you very much' and walk out again. Dailies do – and sometimes afterwards, they won't talk to journalists again.

Mental health and suicide: media guidelines

The Department of Health has produced a useful guide for journalists on reporting mental health and suicide. Called *What's the Story?* (www.shift.org.uk/mediahandbook), its aim is to encourage greater sensitivity and understanding, particularly with regard to the use of appropriate language. For example, terms such as 'psycho' and 'nutter' are discouraged because of their often misplaced stereotypical associations with violence. The guide also advises that it is factually incorrect to refer to someone with a split personality as 'schizophrenic', and that it is preferable to refer to 'people with mental health problems' rather than 'the mentally ill'. In general, it is better to avoid victimising or demonising by saying 'a person with' rather than 'a person suffering from . . .'.

If reporting suicide, it is important that journalists follow guidelines set out in the Press Complaints Commission's editorial code of practice, giving only basic details about the cause of death to avoid encouraging copycats. Journalists are also advised to include a contact number for the Samaritans, if possible, and to note that because suicide was decriminalised in 1961, the commonly misused term 'commit suicide' is inaccurate.

Children

For wonderful and unexpected quotes, go to a child, but go carefully, because interviewing children is more difficult than it looks and is hedged with complications.

The Press Complaints Commission's code is clear:

1 Young people should be free to complete their time at school without unnecessary intrusion.
2 A child under 16 must not be interviewed or photographed on issues involving their own or another child's welfare unless a custodial parent or similarly responsible adult consents.
3 Pupils must not be approached or photographed at school without the permission of the school authorities.

There's also a whole section offering guidance on interviewing/reporting children involved in sex cases.

The hazardous ages in interviewing children are from four to 10. During that time children have a tendency to say yes, being unwilling to contradict an adult who's interviewing them. With teenagers, of course, the opposite can be true. They may delight in defying, shocking or confusing adults.

Questions to younger children shouldn't suggest an answer. Not: 'Did you enjoy that film?' Rather: 'What did you think of that film?' And of course younger children shouldn't be helped with an answer. If they're feeling shy, embarrassed or if they don't understand what you're talking about, they may well answer by saying they don't know. You also must accept they may become tongue-tied because they're transfixed by your ears, your spectacles or something else going on in the room. Try to keep interviews with youngsters short, and avoid noisy places full of distractions and interruptions.

Sarah McCrum and Lotte Hughes of Save the Children have written a booklet, *Interviewing Children* (2nd edition, 2003), full of valuable advice, most of it pure commonsense: listen, don't interrupt, see children as individuals with thoughts and feelings deserving attention, choose where to interview carefully.

Take care with words

Choose your words with care. Even younger teenagers will bridle if asked if they'd 'give a child's perspective on . . .' Call them 'young people'. Young prostitutes may prefer the description 'hostess' or 'sex worker'.

In summary the booklet sets out what children want interviewers to do:

- let them speak for themselves without adult interference;
- treat them as equals;
- see them as individuals with their own thoughts, enthusiasm and concerns;
- let them speak freely;
- value their experiences;
- take their opinions seriously.

Interviewing Children covers where to find children to interview, thoughts on selection, and obtaining permission:

> The wishes and rights of children need to be balanced against those of parents or guardians. But we think that children's wishes and best interests should be paramount – because they have the right to speak out, and adults don't have the right to silence them.
>
> This becomes a thorny issue when you want to talk to minors who are, say, in local government care. They might be living on the street, but still officially in 'care'. Or they could be young offenders in an institution, or under-age soldiers in an army – all situations where adults in authority may say you can't interview the children because they are at risk, or somehow spoken for.

Ask the children

In the UK, the law says that you must get permission from the local authority to interview young people under 18 who are in care. Leave it to the child to decide whether or not they want to be quoted. Adults may try to gag children because they are afraid of what they might say, or afraid it will show them in a bad light. But their classic excuse for trying to stop children being interviewed is that the children are vulnerable and need to be protected. That's rather patronising. The same thing used to be said about women.

When an interview has been set up with children, *Interviewing Children* advises an exploratory visit to prepare the ground, allowing plenty of time for the actual interview, sitting at the children's level and answering the children's questions about yourself and any equipment or shorthand you might be using. There is also advice on drawing out the reluctant, interviewing abroad when using a translator, and ways to end the interview.

Death knocks

Tragedy makes good copy. The best interviewers appreciate this and at the same time sympathise with the people they interview, a fact that comes through clearly again and again from talking to journalists experienced in 'death knocks' or 'fatals'. Former Birmingham *Evening Mail* journalist Sue White says:

> In some ways, doing a fatal is almost as easy as court reporting. You've got to listen, that's the key. You're given the general facts and you get them confirmed. You can sit in with people and they will tell you everything. To be frank, I rather enjoyed interviewing people whose relatives had died in car crashes or traumatic circumstances.

Reporters most often get details of deaths from routine calls to the police, ambulance and fire services. The desk officer provides the basic information: name, address (if these are available), and how the body was found and where. Depending on the time and whether it's a morning, evening or weekly paper or online, the reporter may write up the story so far for the next edition or updating, and go straight out to the house/scene of death. As White recounts:

> If the death had happened overnight, say a 17-year-old boy on a motorbike, I'd write the story for the first edition and then set off, not knowing what I would find. Normally it would be quiet and I'd knock on the door. It would open a crack and someone would answer.
>
> I'd know from the police if the boy lived at home, so – it's an intuitive thing – I'd say: 'Hello, I'm Sue White from the Birmingham *Evening Mail*. We've heard from the police about the dreadful accident last night. Could I come in and have a word with you about it?' Almost everyone would say 'All right'.

Death today is sanitised and tidied away, and few people under 30 have seen a dead body or experienced bereavement. They may not realise that, after a death, relatives are in shock and often have a need to talk freely.

Checking details

White goes on:

> If it was a neighbour who answered, they might not know what to do and would bring the mother or father to the door. It's important to be very, very courteous and understanding. I'd repeat where I was from and that we wanted to check we had all the details correct.
>
> I'd be taken in and sat in the lounge. It would be very quiet, they'd be stunned. I felt if I talked openly, in as friendly and sympathetic a way as possible – one person to another, making it clear I just wanted to confirm some facts – people would give me that information. I was usually right.
>
> What they tell you leads on to further questions. They'd say 'And he was just about to get married', and you'd think the story is getting better. 'Oh, really,' I'd say. They'd tell me about her and I'd ask, 'Would you mind if we went and had a word?' Normally there would be no objection, provided I had appeared sympathetic and understanding.
>
> I always made out I was double-checking, because that way they feel they are not being grilled. It's a sympathetic way of leading them into answering questions and their responses will reveal more of the story. I never felt I was taking advantage of anybody. They want to unburden themselves. It all just flows out.
>
> After I'd established what had happened and that I genuinely wanted to hear about it, the rest of the story would come out. How long he'd had the bike, that he was a leading light in the club and had won trophies, or that he'd had a row with his girlfriend and was on his way to say sorry . . . a tremendous story, I'd think.
>
> If it was a young girl killed in a car crash, I'd ask what sort of car she was driving and they'd say 'Well, it was a new Ford and she did love it.' 'Why?' I'd ask. 'Because her father

> scrimped and saved and put all his money from when he was made redundant . . .' And there's your story.

Think pix

And:

> After a while and they'd gone quiet, I'd say: 'By the way, have you any photographs of him, a nice picture we could put in the paper?' They'd rummage about in the sideboard and bring out a choice of pictures. I'd know which was the one the paper would use, but I'd take them all, to make sure the *Express and Star* [the opposition] didn't get them. They'd do the same to us.

Always promise you'll take good care of the pix and plan to return them personally – and mean it. Your paper's reputation is involved. Ensure the photos are identified with name and address written in a *soft* – say 2B – pencil on the back, not with a ballpoint pen, and do make it plain when passing any photographs onto the picture desk or production how important it is that they must be returned. Increasingly, people have digital photographs so also ask them to email you a copy.

If journalists from competing papers arrive on the doorstep at the same time, they'll do a joint interview and share the pix, perhaps phoning back separately for additional quotes. If the opposition gets there first and takes all the pictures offered, the relatives will be able to find some more from somewhere, but they may not be as good.

Suspicious circumstances

'If the fatal was something good like a murder, I'd go straight out to the address I'd been given by the police or the ambulance men,' says White. 'If it wasn't clear how the child or person died and no one had been charged, you're free to report it. So I'd knock on the door.'

Relatives of someone who has died in suspicious circumstances are just as shocked as relatives of someone who has died in an accident, but there are usually added emotions, ranging from anger or shame to blame and guilt. So the doorstep reaction is less certain.

Some slam the door in your face but it didn't happen very often to me. With one story we had to track down the relatives of three members of a family found gassed in a car in their garage. A colleague went to see one set of grandparents and I went to the other. I had a feeling it was not going to be good.

She didn't slam the door but started shouting at me on the doorstep, then chased me down the front garden path yelling 'Sod off!' I think the *Express and Star* had got to her before we did. So I went to the neighbours.

If the relative is incensed, it's wise to start with neighbours on the same side of the road but not visible from the relative's house. It's rare that neighbours can't give you something.

If a relative who has refused an interview then sees the reporter talking to a neighbour, they may try to prevent the interview.

One man who wouldn't talk bawled at me, so – because you don't come away without a story – I went across the road, but a few doors away, so he couldn't see me. He stormed after me into this bloke's garden, shouting: 'You can't do this – I'm going to call the police.' It's very important to be polite. If you retaliate you lose it. So I said 'Yes, actually I can', and I went on interviewing.

Once the initial shock has passed, the reaction of most people to a relative's preventable death is to wish for recognition of the dead person's life and to hope that their death has not been in vain. A sympathetic interview and accurate report can meet both these wishes and often brings an added journalistic reward, as in this story from Sue White:

A 24-year-old woman with two young children had to have a heart transplant. Her husband had died the year before from a brain haemorrhage. She was a really nice, quiet, gentle woman and I interviewed her at her mother's house before the operation.

After she'd had the new heart I checked back every day with relatives and the hospital. The operation had been fine but a week later she caught an infection and died. Her husband had been buried in his wedding suit and, talking to the grandmother, it came out that the 24-year-old was to be buried in her wedding dress. Superb.

You may wince at that last word, but you must recognise that the journalist would not have been welcomed into the house three times if she hadn't been a sympathetic, understanding reporter and that what she wrote was accurate and had passed intense scrutiny. It's fairly certain that the stories comforted the grieving relatives who treasure the cuttings.

Part of the job

However much you may hate this type of interviewing, it's part of a journalist's job. A regional newspaper reporter found this out the hard way when he was asked to contact a famous former football manager whose son had killed himself. He refused. He said it would damage the close personal relationship he had with the manager, and he was not prepared to accept an alternative job, which he considered a demotion.

An employment tribunal decided against him, judging that the editor and the paper had acted reasonably throughout. 'Although the circumstances were tragic for the former manager this was a matter of national importance and it was an opportunity for a local paper to obtain a scoop.' The reporter lost his claim for unfair dismissal.

Self-interest dictates that local paper journalists dealing with a local tragedy proceed circumspectly. It's a different matter with the national press covering a national disaster. Fiercely competitive reporters descend and do what's necessary to get the story and accompanying pix. They know they're unlikely to return to the same street in the next five years and it's a licence to behave badly – and some do.

A trainee on a tabloid Sunday was told: 'There's been a murder. Go and get an interview and we'll send a photographer.' The two of them talked their way in, got the interview and the photographs. The photographer then became incredibly aggressive, so much so that the woman threw them both out. Afterwards, the trainee asked 'Why did you do that?' 'Well,' said the photographer, 'the next paper that comes along won't get in.'

The bereaved as campaigner

If a bereavement later becomes linked to a campaign, for example parents raising awareness about meningitis symptoms after the death of their child, the interviewer needs to use a more businesslike approach. Here, the bereaved want to be taken seriously rather than sympathised with. They are on a mission.

You need to be well clued-up as regards the relevant disease or condition – the internet has enabled people often to become obsessively knowledgeable, and they won't warm to you if you haven't bothered to do your research beforehand. Luckily for the interviewer, though, people in these circumstances are usually incredibly driven and eager to answer all your questions.

PRs and two-handers

The truism couldn't be truer: two's company, three's a crowd. PRs sitting in on interviews can be a nuisance. Playing gooseberry, they sour that special one-to-one relationship that's at the heart of a good interview. Probably the best way to take it is as a compliment. You're so good that a watchdog is needed.

One on two

Royals, government ministers, many celebrities and certain chief executives of multinationals always have a PR present as well as a recorder running. With a smaller organisation, when a PR sits in, it's probably because the interviewee is inexperienced or very nervous.

Alan Russell, who has worked in PR on both sides of the Atlantic, says some clients are so intimidated by journalists that they ask PRs to sit in for protection. 'But,' he says, 'the PR has to sit there absolutely stumm. It's very tempting to offer answers when you feel your client is not doing very well, but you have to fight against it.'

With the exception of royal and government press officers, PRs who wish to sit in and are doing their job properly will ask if you mind their being present. Unless it was a condition of the interview, you are entitled to reply 'Yes, I do', but it's probably wisest not to. The essential thing is to ensure they are sitting in full view. If they say modestly 'I'll just tuck myself away here' (behind you), beware. This means they can signal to the interviewee when danger threatens, when to change tack, when to produce a red herring.

You must ensure you can see both of them. Ideally, fix it so that they are facing you and eye contact between them is restricted. Some journalists, when offered a chair, accept it and stay where they are put. Not always wise. All you have to say is: 'Do you mind? I'd be much happier over here.' There's no need to give a reason. Or you can make a joke of it saying: 'I want to keep my eyes on both of you!' These are all accepted manoeuvres in a constantly played game.

The positive side of having a PR present is that they can be useful, adding points of detail that the interviewee doesn't have to hand or saving a lot of time by agreeing to provide missing information later. They may leave the room to fetch necessary paperwork. That's your opportunity. If you're really lucky, the PR will be called away to the phone during the interview. Now that's worth thinking about.

Journalists depend on PRs more than most of us like to admit, which makes the PR love–hate relationship with journalists easy to understand. Because PRs understand the way journalists think, they are able to feed journalists with ideas, copy and pictures specifically tailored for individual readerships. On the journalist's part this makes for dependence.

Because they understand the way journalists think, PRs are able to advise their clients how to resist interviewers' wiles. 'Never do an interview at home,' they counsel. 'Gives away too much about you. Try an anonymous hotel room instead . . . It's important to come prepared for questions on . . . Beware the tricky question, based on rumours . . .' On the journalist's part this makes for intense irritation.

Interviewing PRs

When interviewing PRs, be straightforward and direct. They understand journalists far too well to be fooled by attempts at guile. They've sat in on too many interviews where the journalists have missed the real story to be impressed. Most importantly, they have good memories. Not selective, like journalists, but based on letters and cuttings: what we said and what we delivered.

Two on one

There may come occasions when you find yourself doing a two-handed interview: two journalists, one interviewee. This may be because time is limited and the interviewee decides to talk to feature writers from, say, a weekly and a monthly publication at the same time. Since you're not immediate competitors, this is possible though not desirable. You may be a specialist interviewing someone so prestigious that your editor (not a specialist in your area) wants to join you. Or you may be one of two specialists from the same paper coming at the interviewee from different angles.

In each instance it's important to work out together beforehand how the questioning will be shared and who will start. Maybe equally – for example, 'I'll ask the first question, you ask the second.' Then you have to agree how many follow-up questions are admissible. This can be tricky for the interviewee, since the questioning may swing wildly from subject to subject. So give them fair warning. The alternative is to agree to interview, say, 10 minutes at a time.

Problems arise if one interviewer from a competing publication breaks the agreement to share interviewing time equally and hogs the questioning. If you're by nature kind, considerate and polite, then ask to be sent on an assertiveness course. You're there to get a story, not to let the other reporter get their story.

Three-, four- and five-handers are definitely to be avoided if possible. One hapless feature writer from a teenage magazine found at the last minute that her one-on-one interview with Tom Cruise had turned into a four-hander: herself and three middle-aged Dutchmen. The film involved flying stunts and, despite the poor woman's best efforts, the conversation turned technical and she was frozen out while the men discussed F-14s. Putting yourself in her position, it's tough. Put yourself in Tom Cruise's position, and it's a great relief. She'd wanted to ask him whether he preferred Y-fronts or boxer shorts.

Ah, journalism.

12
Law and ethics

Wynford Hicks

If you want to be a competent professional interviewer, talent, skill and experience are essential – but they are not enough. You must also know and understand the law as it applies to journalists and be familiar with the professional and ethical issues of journalism, particularly as defined by the Press Complaints Commission (PCC) in their editorial code of practice.

The PCC code and a similar one issued by the National Union of Journalists (NUJ) are included in this chapter, but there is no such concise and convenient summary of the law as it applies to journalists. Even a complete chapter on it would be inadequate: you need a good textbook, such as *McNae's Essential Law for Journalists*, now published by Oxford University Press.

Make sure you get hold of the latest edition, since media law changes constantly. As the preface to the 19th edition (published in 2007) notes: 'The flood of legislation that has been recorded in the preface of recent editions of *McNae* has continued unabated.'

Libel

Libel is the most powerful constraint on journalists. Possibly because it is so tough, its scope is exaggerated by some people – even some of those who offer advice to journalists. For example, two books on interviewing (*Interviewing for Journalists* by Joan Clayton and *Interviewing Techniques for Writers & Researchers* by Susan Dunne) make the misleading claim that true and accurate statements can be libellous.

Justification

In fact, as *McNae* points out: 'It is a complete defence to a libel action . . . to prove that the words complained of are substantially true.' This defence is known as 'justification'.

The 'Venetian blind'

The confusion probably comes from the notorious difficulty journalists face in proving the truth of the words complained of – as is shown by a string of cases where libel juries have got it wrong. For example, writing in the *Guardian*, Geoffrey Wheatcroft recalled what Labour Party wits called the 'Venetian blind':

> In 1957, an article in the *Spectator* skittishly suggested that three Labour politicians had been drinking a good deal at a socialist conference in Venice. The three, Aneurin Bevan, Richard Crossman and Morgan Phillips, sued, testified on oath to their sobriety, and won large damages.
>
> Fifteen years later, Crossman boasted (in my presence) that they had indeed all been toping heavily, and that at least one of them had been blind drunk.

The fact is that in libel cases where justification is claimed, it is for the defendant to prove the truth of the words complained of – there is no presumption of innocence, as in other legal proceedings.

Other defences

There are other defences to libel. The main ones are:

- fair comment (not 'fair' in the sense of 'just' but comment based on an honestly held opinion);
- privilege (statements made, e.g. in court or at a public meeting);
- accord and satisfaction (e.g. the publication of a correction and apology, accepted by the plaintiff);
- offer of amends (e.g. in cases where the libel is accidental).

Others include:

- that the plaintiff has died – the dead are not protected by the law of libel, which explains why the death of Robert Maxwell was followed by a tidal wave of hostile comment (while he was alive he intimidated the press by constantly issuing libel writs);
- that the plaintiff agreed to the publication – a signed statement from them, if you could obtain one, would obviously do the trick.

Two other points weigh heavily against the defendant. First, it is not necessary for the plaintiff to prove that the defendant *intended* to libel them. For example, by printing an interviewee's libellous comment on a third party – without in any way endorsing it – you publish the libel.

Also, the test of whether a statement is defamatory has nothing to do with the meaning intended by the person who made it or published it. Instead it's the meaning that 'a reasonable person' would understand it to have. Innuendo – a hidden meaning – is dangerous. For example, 'tired and emotional', *Private Eye*'s traditional euphemism for drunk, might well be considered to have this meaning even if the journalist using the phrase meant it literally.

Second, it is not necessary to prove that the words complained of have actually damaged the reputation of the plaintiff – merely that they *tended* to do so.

A statement can be defamatory of a person if it tends to do any one of the following:

- expose them to hatred, ridicule or contempt;
- cause them to be shunned or avoided;
- lower them in the estimation of right-thinking members of society generally;
- disparage them in their business, trade, office or profession.

So, faced with this legal minefield, what is the journalist to do? A very common cause of libel actions is the failure to apply professional standards of accuracy and fairness. Most libel actions can be avoided.

Make and keep accurate notes

Some of the cases cited in *McNae* are hair-raising. For example, when in 1997 the *Sunday Times* was trying to prove the truth of a story about

Albert Reynolds, the former Irish prime minister, the reporter who wrote the story told the court he had no notes. 'I was not in note-taking mode,' he said.

Having made accurate notes, keep them and any tapes for one year after your story is published. The Defamation Act 1996 reduced the time within which an action must be started to one year after publication.

Check the cuttings – and what you're told in the interview

Remember that cuttings are only a starting point: they should never be assumed to be accurate, so check the content with the interviewee.

If a cutting contains a libellous statement and you republish it, this is called a fresh publication – and creates a fresh cause of action. The plaintiff can now sue you for libel whether or not they sued the original publisher.

Then, if your interviewee says something defamatory about another person, can it be proved to be true? Will your interviewee stand by their statement and can they back it up to the satisfaction of a jury?

Legal advice

Libel experts make various suggestions about how you can reduce the chance of being sued or at least improve your chances of winning in court. One is to persuade your interviewee to make a signed statement confirming what they say; if they die or change their minds, you have something to back up your story.

Another is to have your copy – or the factual parts of it – checked by the person or organisation concerned. This idea runs counter to journalistic tradition (and in some confrontational stories is clearly impractical) but it is worth considering.

Finally, if you think your story is potentially libellous, you (or your editor) should take legal advice. On some publications, page proofs are routinely legalled (checked by a lawyer) before publication.

Slander

Whereas libel is defamation in permanent or broadcast form, slander is usually spoken. In theory a journalist can slander somebody merely by asking questions – but this is rare.

Malicious falsehood

This is publication of a false statement likely to damage somebody. By contrast with libel, the plaintiff must prove that the statement is untrue and that it is made maliciously.

Copyright

Copyright particularly concerns interviewers in two ways: first, when you use cuttings, you must not lift large chunks verbatim from the original story. As well as being bad practice professionally – the material is unchecked, your readers (who may have seen the original) are being short-changed – this is a breach of copyright.

There is now copyright in the spoken word as soon as it is recorded (with or without the speaker's permission) and it belongs to the speaker. When somebody agrees to be interviewed, they are assumed to agree that their words can be recorded and published. But if they do not give their consent, there may be a breach of copyright.

Trespass, harassment, breach of confidence

Although there is no law of privacy, legal action to protect it is possible under other headings, such as trespass, harassment and breach of confidence.

The traditional warning 'Trespassers will be prosecuted' is something of an empty threat. First, trespass is defined as injuring land, goods or the person: merely walking onto a person's property is unlikely to do much damage. Second, it is a civil rather than a criminal matter: the owner sues for damages. But the owner is entitled to ask trespassers to leave private property – and to use reasonable force to eject them – so if you're asked to leave, you must do so.

Many apparently 'public' places are in fact private property. For example, a shopping centre and the forecourt of a bus station are obvious places to conduct vox pop interviews – journalists should not be intimidated from entering them. But security guards acting for the owner are legally entitled to ask you to leave.

Harassment is now recognised as an offence under the Protection from Harassment Act 1997. Although harassment is not defined in the Act, it is defined in the PCC code (see pages 194–200).

The law of confidentiality bans the publication of material that has been gathered in confidence, as when a domestic servant reveals private information about their employer. This was the law used in 1989 in the case of Bill Goodwin, a trainee reporter working for *Engineer* magazine.

Goodwin received information from a source inside an engineering company and phoned them to check it. The company's response was to obtain an injunction restraining the *Engineer* from publishing the story and an order requiring Goodwin to hand over notes that would reveal his source. When he refused, he was fined £5,000 – though in 1996 the European Court of Human Rights decided that the order and the fine violated his right to freedom of expression.

Codes of conduct/practice

The two most important codes for print journalists are those of the NUJ and the PCC.

The NUJ code of conduct

The NUJ has had a code of conduct for its members since the late 1930s. For a time during the 1980s attempts were made to enforce the code by considering complaints against individual journalists. But this practice was not widely supported and has been abandoned. Now the code is seen by the NUJ as a target for journalists to aim for rather than a means to punish those who fail to abide by it.

A journalist:

1. at all times upholds and defends the principle of media freedom, the right of freedom of expression and the right of the public to be informed;
2. strives to ensure that information disseminated is honestly conveyed, accurate and fair;
3. does her/his utmost to correct harmful inaccuracies;
4. differentiates between fact and opinion;
5. obtains material by honest, straightforward and open means, with the exception of investigations that are both overwhelmingly in the public interest and which involve evidence that cannot be obtained by straightforward means;
6. does nothing to intrude into anybody's private life, grief or distress unless justified by overriding consideration of the public interest;
7. protects the identity of sources who supply information in confidence and material gathered in the course of her/his work;
8. resists threats or any other inducements to influence, distort or suppress information;
9. takes no unfair personal advantage of information gained in the course of her/his duties before the information is public knowledge;
10. produces no material likely to lead to hatred or discrimination on the grounds of a person's age, gender, race, colour, creed, legal status, disability, marital status or sexual orientation;
11. does not by way of statement, voice or appearance endorse by advertisement any commercial product or service save for the promotion of her/his own work or of the medium by which she/he is employed;
12. avoids plagiarism.

The PCC code of practice

The PCC was set up by the industry in 1991 in response to the Calcutt committee's tough warning that, if the press did not clean up its act, it would face statutory regulation. The code of practice drafted by a committee of editors was based on an existing code of the Newspaper Publishers Association and proposals from the Calcutt committee and the former Press Council. It has since been amended in response to various events, such as the furore over alleged press harassment of Princess Diana. (The version reproduced here dates from 1 August 2007.)

1 *Accuracy*

(i) The press must take care not to publish inaccurate, misleading or distorted information, including pictures.

(ii) A significant inaccuracy, misleading statement or distortion once recognised must be corrected, promptly and with due prominence, and – where appropriate – an apology published.

(iii) The press, whilst free to be partisan, must distinguish clearly between comment, conjecture and fact.

(iv) A publication must report fairly and accurately the outcome of an action for defamation to which it has been a party, unless an agreed settlement states otherwise, or an agreed statement is published.

2 *Opportunity to reply*

A fair opportunity to reply to inaccuracies must be given when reasonably called for.

3 **Privacy*

(i) Everyone is entitled to respect for his or her private and family life, home, health and correspondence, including digital communications. Editors will be expected to justify intrusions into any individual's private life without consent.

(ii) It is unacceptable to photograph individuals in a private place without their consent.

Note: private places are public or private property where there is a reasonable expectation of privacy.

4 **Harassment*

(i) Journalists must not engage in intimidation, harassment or persistent pursuit.

(ii) They must not persist in questioning, telephoning, pursuing or photographing individuals once asked to desist; nor remain on their property when asked to leave and must not follow them.

(iii) Editors must ensure these principles are observed by those working for them and take care not to use non-compliant material from other sources.

5 *Intrusion into grief or shock*

(i) In cases involving personal grief or shock, enquiries and approaches must be made with sympathy and discretion and publication handled sensitively. This should not restrict the right to report legal proceedings, such as inquests.

(ii) When reporting suicide, care should be taken to avoid excessive detail about the method used.

6 **Children*

(i) Young people should be free to complete their time at school without unnecessary intrusion.

(ii) A child under 16 must not be interviewed or photographed on issues involving their own or another child's welfare unless a custodial parent or similarly responsible adult consents.

(iii) Pupils must not be approached or photographed at school without the permission of the school authorities.

(iv) Minors must not be paid for material involving children's welfare, nor parents or guardians for material about their children or wards unless it is clearly in the child's interest.

(v) Editors must not use the fame, notoriety or position of a parent or guardian as sole justification for publishing details of a child's private life.

7 **Children in sex cases*

1 The press must not, even if legally free to do so, identify children under the age of 16 who are victims or witnesses in cases involving sex offences.

2 In any press report of a case involving a sexual offence against a child:

(i) the child must not be identified;
(ii) the adult may be identified;
(iii) the word 'incest' must not be used where a child victim might be identified;
(iv) care must be taken that nothing in the report implies the relationship between the accused and the child.

8 **Hospitals*

(i) Journalists must identify themselves and obtain permission from a responsible executive before entering non-public areas of hospitals or similar institutions to pursue enquiries.

(ii) The restrictions on intruding into privacy are particularly relevant to enquiries about individuals in hospitals or similar institutions.

9 **Reporting of crime*

(i) Relatives or friends of persons convicted or accused of crime should not generally be identified without their consent, unless they are genuinely relevant to the story.

(ii) Particular regard should be paid to the potentially vulnerable position of children who witness, or are victims of, crime. This should not restrict the right to report legal proceedings.

10 **Clandestine devices and subterfuge*

(i) The press must not seek to obtain or publish material acquired by using hidden cameras or clandestine listening devices; or by intercepting private or mobile telephone calls, messages or emails; or by the unauthorised removal of documents or photographs; or by accessing digitally held private information without consent.

(ii) Engaging in misrepresentation or subterfuge, including by agents or intermediaries, can generally be justified only in the public interest and then only when the material cannot be obtained by other means.

11 *Victims of sexual assault*

The press must not identify victims of sexual assault or publish material likely to contribute to such identification unless there is adequate justification and they are legally free to do so.

12 *Discrimination*

(i) The press must avoid prejudicial or pejorative reference to an individual's race, colour, religion, gender, sexual orientation or to any physical or mental illness or disability.

(ii) Details of an individual's race, colour, religion, sexual orientation, physical or mental illness or disability must be avoided unless genuinely relevant to the story.

13 *Financial journalism*

(i) Even where the law does not prohibit it, journalists must not use for their own profit financial information they receive in advance of its general publication, nor should they pass such information to others.

(ii) They must not write about shares or securities in whose performance they know that they or their close families have a significant financial interest, without disclosing the interest to the editor or financial editor.

(iii) They must not buy or sell, either directly or through nominees or agents, shares or securities about which they have written recently or about which they intend to write in the near future.

14 *Confidential sources*

Journalists have a moral obligation to protect confidential sources of information.

15 *Witness payments in criminal trials*

(i) No payment or offer of payment to a witness – or any person who may reasonably be expected to be called as a witness – should be made in any case once proceedings are active as defined by the Contempt of Court Act 1981.

This prohibition lasts until the suspect has been freed unconditionally by police without charge or bail or the proceedings are otherwise discontinued; or has entered a guilty plea to the court; or, in the event of a not guilty plea the court has announced its verdict.

(ii) *Where proceedings are not yet active but are likely and foreseeable, editors must not make or offer payment to any person who may reasonably be expected to be called as a witness, unless the information concerned ought demonstrably to be published in the public interest and there is an overriding need to make or promise payment for this to be done; and all reasonable steps have been taken to ensure no financial dealings influence the evidence those witnesses give. In no circumstances should such payment be conditional on the outcome of a trial.

(iii) *Any payment or offer of payment made to a person later cited to give evidence in proceedings must be disclosed to the prosecution and defence. The witness must be advised of this requirement.

16 **Payment to criminals*

(i) Payment or offers of payment for stories, pictures or information, which seek to exploit a particular crime or to glorify or glamorise crime in general, must not be made directly or via agents to convicted or confessed criminals or to their associates – who may include family, friends and colleagues.

(ii) Editors invoking the public interest to justify payment or offers would need to demonstrate that there was good reason to believe the public interest would be served. If, despite payment, no public interest emerged, then the material should not be published.

The public interest

There may be exceptions to the clauses marked * where they can be demonstrated to be in the public interest.

1 The public interest includes, but is not confined to:
   (i) detecting or exposing crime or serious impropriety;
   (ii) protecting public health and safety;
   (iii) preventing the public from being misled by an action or statement of an individual or organisation.

2 There is a public interest in freedom of expression itself.

3 Whenever the public interest is invoked, the PCC will require editors to demonstrate fully how the public interest was served.

4 The PCC will consider the extent to which material is already in the public domain, or will become so.

5 In cases involving children under 16, editors must demonstrate an exceptional public interest to override the normally paramount interest of the child.

Other issues

So much for media law and the professional codes. But what about the issues they don't cover – and your own personal ethical standards? Are there things that some interviewers do that seem to you either morally wrong or at least dubious?

The buy-up interview

For example, what about the buy-up interview, when a publication pays the interviewee for an exclusive? This is often disparaged by the use of the emotive phrase 'chequebook journalism' – some people claim that paying for stories is both lazy and potentially corrupt. They say that journalists should not pay the people they interview because (a) it makes the job too easy and (b) it raises doubts about the authenticity of what is said (as well as being unfair competition for poorer publications).

Before you endorse this view, consider two points. First, look at the situation from the interviewee's point of view. If they have a story to tell, why shouldn't they sell it? If it's a good story, the publication stands to profit and the interviewer gets a credit as well as being paid. Why shouldn't the interviewee make something out of it?

My view of 'chequebook journalism' changed radically when I was asked by a lawyer to negotiate the sale of an exclusive interview on behalf of a political activist released from jail in a foreign country. The person concerned wanted to be interviewed by a sympathetic journalist. But, having just come out of jail, he also needed money. So – his decision – the story went to the highest bidder, a Sunday tabloid.

Part of the deal, incidentally, was that we had a limited degree of copy approval: the page proofs of the story were to be checked by us to ensure that the interviewee had not accidentally named, and so compromised, other political activists. This, of course, would not have been possible in a free-for-all, such as an open press conference.

Second, compare the buy-up interview with the serialisation of a book, particularly a ghosted book (where the 'author' is interviewed by a journalist who effectively writes the book). In ethical terms, what's the difference? Yet nobody suggests that the 'author' of a ghosted book shouldn't be paid for 'writing' it or that they shouldn't be paid a second time when it is serialised.

The law of copyright is useful here: it is a reminder that a person normally 'owns' their own words. Thus in a society regulated by money it is surely reasonable that a person should be able to sell an exclusive interview – and therefore, logically, that a publication should be able to buy it.

Freebies

'Inducements' (offers of bribes?) are mentioned in the NUJ code, but neither it nor the PCC code refers explicitly to freebies: lunches, trips abroad, cars on loan and other goodies provided to journalists by organisations keen to attract editorial coverage for their products and services. As with 'inducements', the issue is clear-cut: a journalist must not allow them to influence the performance of their professional duties.

Some publications ban their staff from accepting freebies, but this is rare: the majority have to learn to live with the fact that Christmas comes more than once a year. And, in general, this is something they're quite good at: the robust, cynical culture of British journalism encourages hacks to sup politely with the devil – then complain in print that the supper was far too hot.

Entertaining

Payment for entertaining rarely poses an ethical problem: when journalists conduct interviews over a drink, who pays for it is usually incidental. But if the interviewee pays, the journalist should obviously not then claim the drinks on expenses.

Privacy

Of all the issues journalists must face, privacy is the most important: it features prominently in the professional codes, and by being included in the European convention on human rights it has become part of the UK legal landscape. And it is the issue that most concerns the politicians, academics, celebrities and other non-journalists who would like to see a more regulated rather than a freer press.

Some politicians are exceptions to the trend: ex-Liberal Democrat leader Paddy Ashdown, for example, told the *Times* when it serialised his diaries in 2000 that he was not in favour of a privacy law. 'I fear it would only serve to protect the rich and powerful,' he said – making the obvious point.

There have been – still are – abuses of people's privacy: reporters on trivial stories doorstepping; bereaved relatives being pursued; hospital patients having unwelcome visitors. But some of the famous/notorious cases of 'press intrusion' aren't quite so straightforward.

The best known case is that of Princess Diana. In the emotive aftermath of her death in a Paris car crash it was even suggested that its 'cause' was harassment by press photographers. This canard was disposed of by the French inquest which established that Diana's driver was drunk at the time of the crash.

More generally, it is difficult for someone in Diana's position to play the privacy card if they spend so much time trying to manipulate the media.

The two most flagrant examples of this were her secret collaboration with Andrew Morton in the writing of *Diana: Her True Story* and the notorious Panorama interview in which she announced her intention of becoming the 'Queen of Hearts'.

The same point applies to politicians. Those who electioneer by means of happy-family pix of wife/husband and little ones can hardly complain when the mask is torn away to reveal MP in bed with hooker. Also, if politicians are to be allowed their 'privacy', it will be invoked to cover not just their sexual activities but their financial ones as well.

The other side of the channel provides an awful warning here. French politicians are traditionally allowed their 'privacy' – so the voters usually find out about their various misdemeanours only after their death.

There is a paradox in the current obsession with 'privacy' as an issue. For never before have interviewees – celebrities, royals, politicians, sport stars and ordinary people – been so ready to reveal themselves via the media to the world. The audience demands and enjoys more and more access; their targets are more than ever eager to oblige. Politicians publish their diaries, sports stars their ghosted autobiographies, both full of intimate detail. Celebrities queue up to be paid to appear in magazines like *Hello!* and *OK!*; ordinary people queue up to appear on programmes like *Big Brother*. In this situation, blaming the media for abusing people's privacy misses the point. Much of this 'abuse' is really self-abuse.

But the practical issue remains: how far should you go in 'intruding on', 'harassing' and 'pursuing' those you wish to interview? The only possible answer is: it depends on the story. It's not that the end would justify the means if the means were intrinsically evil, but it's reasonable to balance the public good against the private annoyance.

Entrapment

This is the old tabloid trick where the undercover journalist approaches the alleged celebrity drug user/dealer, pretending to sell/use drugs, then writes up the story. In most cases the only justification for the trick is to sell more newspapers. In the honey trap, sex (or the promise of it) is the bait.

There are signs that, while the trick continues to sell papers, it does less damage to the celebrities involved. Rugby star Lawrence Dallaglio, victim of the *News of the World* in 1999, was soon reinstated in the England team; the Earl of Hardwicke, caught by a *News of the World* drugs sting, was later told by the judge: 'Were it not for that elaborate sting you would not, I accept, have committed these particular offences' – and escaped a jail sentence.

The ex-tabloid editor Roy Greenslade, now an academic who also writes on media issues for the *Guardian*, called the Hardwicke case a landmark moment with the message: 'Drugs may be bad. Drug-dealing may be worse. But journalistic subterfuge is even worse still. By extension therefore tabloid investigators are greater sinners than drug-dealers.'

Attributing quotes

Quotes should be attributed to one named individual. (Avoid suggesting that two or more people used identical words unless they are a music-hall act.) This gives your story authenticity – indeed the stronger and more vivid the quote, the more the reader will want to know who said it.

There are exceptions to this rule. It is general practice not to identify press officers. Their job is to speak on behalf of an organisation so they are its 'spokesman' or 'spokeswoman' (please not, except in parody, 'spokesperson'). But, given the choice, quote a named individual in an organisation rather than its press officer.

This exception has traditionally applied to political briefings, such as those of the parliamentary lobby (specialist reporters covering parliament) by the prime minister's press secretary. But anonymous political briefings are increasingly criticised – particularly where they involve character assassination of ministers who have fallen out of favour.

Indeed in both politics and general news it is now argued that pejorative blind quotes are journalistically unethical. Some British journalists now favour the approach of American broadsheet papers such as the *New York Times*, whose stylebook says: 'Anonymity must not become a cloak for attacks on people . . .' It is hard to disagree.

In some stories, interviewees can't be named because the consequences for them would be devastating: if identified, they would lose their job or their marriage would collapse, and so on. But if you can't name people, try to avoid giving them false names. It is silly to write 'Darren Smith (not his real name)' or 'Darren Smith' with a footnote that says 'The names in this article have been changed'.

Why not simply write 'Darren ——'? Then the reader gets the idea that you're not identifying him and it doesn't matter whether he's actually called Darren or not.

Appendix 1
Miles Kington on celebrity interviews

Q. What is an interview?

A. An interview is an encounter between an unknown person and a famous person, for which the unknown person gets paid but the celebrity does not.

Q. Why should a celebrity undergo this ordeal?

A. To keep in touch with the public while only having to meet one of them. To put straight mistakes made by the previous interviewer. To publicise a book or film. Because he has been told to.

Q. What does the interviewer get out of it?

A. An autograph for his children.

Q. What does it mean when an interviewer says: 'He paused and thought deeply before replying'?

A. It means the celebrity is trying to remember the answer he always gives to this question.

Q. Does he always give the same answers?

A. Yes.

Q. Why?

A. Because he is always asked the same questions.

Q. How does an interviewer prepare for an interview?

A. He looks up cuttings of previous interviews with the celebrity to see what kind of questions have been asked before.

Q. And then?

A. He asks them again.

Q. What if the interviewer actually does ask different, new questions?
A. The celebrity pauses and thinks deeply, then gives the same old answers.

Q. What is the question most often asked in interviews?
A. 'What sort of difference has fame made to your private life?'

Q. What is the answer to that question?
A. 'It means I have to suffer interviews by odious little nerks like you.'

Q. Does he actually say that?
A. No. He says: 'I have very little private life, but I owe everything to the public, and never resent their intrusion.'

Q. Does the celebrity manage to correct mistakes made by previous interviewers?
A. Yes.

Q. Does this make him happy?
A. No. A new interviewer always makes new mistakes.

Q. What is the difference between a good interviewer and a bad interviewer?
A. A bad interviewer, when writing his piece, always mentions where it took place. 'As we took tea together in the Ritz', or 'Sitting in his elegant work-room, hung with Hockneys' . . .

Q. Are there any other kinds of interview?
A. Yes, the *Radio Times* interview. This always takes place during the actual production of the star's programme, as if to create the impression that the interviewer is talking to him during the white-hot moment of creation.

Q. And is this the impression created?
A. No. We get the impression that the star is too busy to see the interviewer.

Q. How does the interviewer describe the celebrity?
A. As smaller than I had expected.

Q. What do celebrities most like talking about?
A. Their new books or films. But they find this difficult.

Q. Why?
A. Because interviewers prefer talking about their old books and films.

Q. How long does an interview take?
A. About an hour less than the interview contrives to suggest.

Q. Why do so many interviewers end with 'And there, regretfully, I had to leave it'?
A. Because he is being kicked out.

Q. Why?
A. Because someone else is waiting to interview the celebrity. And there, regretfully, we shall have to leave it.

(Miles Kington, the *Independent*, 12 June 1987. Used with permission of the *Independent*.)

Appendix 2
Madonna interviewed as never before

'Are you a bold hussy-woman that feasts on men who are tops?' – 'Yes, yes, this brings to the surface my longings.'

In 1996, Madonna spoke to Hungarian magazine *Blikk*. The questions were asked in Hungarian and translated into English. Madonna's replies were then translated into Hungarian. The interview was published in Hungarian and finally translated back into English. When *Time* magazine reproduced this journalistic gem, it commented: 'To say that something was lost in the process is to be wildly ungrateful for all that was gained.' (These extracts, incidentally, are plucked from cyberspace.)

Blikk: Madonna, Budapest says hello with arms that are spread-eagled. Did you have a visit here that was agreeable? Are you in good odour? You are the biggest fan of our young people who hear your musical productions and like to move their bodies in response.

Madonna: Thank you for saying these compliments [holds up hands]. Please stop with taking sensationalist photographs until I have removed my garments for all to see [laughs]. This is a joke I have made.

Blikk: Madonna, let's cut toward the hunt. Are you a bold hussy-woman that feasts on men who are tops?

Madonna: Yes, yes, this is certainly something that brings to the surface my longings. In America it is not considered to be mentally ill when a woman advances on her prey in a discotheque setting with hardy cocktails present. And there is a more normal attitude toward leather play-tops that also makes my day.

Blikk: Tell us this how you met Carlos, your love servant who is reputed? Did you know he was heaven-sent right off the stick?

Or were you dating many other people in your bed at the same time?

Madonna: No, he was the only one I was dating in my bed then, so it is a scientific fact that the baby was made in my womb using him. But as regards those questions, enough! I am a woman and not a test-mouse! Carlos is an everyday person who is in the orbit of a star who is being muscle-trained by him, not a sex machine.

Blikk: May we talk about your other 'baby' your movie, then? Please do not be denying that the similarities between you and the real Evita are grounded in basis. Power, money, tasty-food, Grammys – all these elements are afoot.

Madonna: What is up in the air with you? Evita never was winning a Grammy!

Blikk: Perhaps not. But as to your film, in trying to bring your reputation along a rocky road, can you make people forget the bad explosions of *Who's That Girl?* and *Shanghai Surprise?*

Madonna: I am a tip-top starlet. That is the job that I am paid to do.

Blikk: OK, here's a question from left space. What was your book *Slut* about?

Madonna: It was called *Sex*, my book.

Blikk: Not in Hungary. Here it was called *Slut*. How did it come to publish? Were you lovemaking with an about-town printer? Do you prefer making suggestive literature to fast-selling CDs?

Madonna: These are different facets to my career highway. I am preferring only to become respected all over the map as a 100 per cent artist.

Blikk: There is much interest in you from this geographical region, so I must ask this final questions. How many Hungarian men have you dated in bed? Are they No 1? How are they comparing to Argentine men, who are famous for being tip-top as well?

Madonna: Well, to avoid aggravating global tension, I won't say. It's a tie [laughs]. No, no, I am serious now. See here I am working like a canine all the way around the clock! I am too busy even to try the goulash that makes your country for the record books.

Blikk: Thank you for your candid chitchat.

Madonna: No problem, friend who is a girl.

(*Evening Standard*, 14 August 1998)

Appendix 3
Nothing to say

'You can tell your paper,' the great man said,
'I refused an interview.
I have nothing to say on the question, sir;
Nothing to say to you.'

And then he talked till the sun went down
And the chickens went to roost;
And he seized the collar of the poor young man,
And never his hold he loosed.

And the sun went down and the moon came up,
And he talked till the dawn of day;
Though he said, 'On this subject mentioned by you,
I have nothing whatever to say.'

And down the reporter dropped to sleep
And flat on the floor he lay;
And the last he heard was the great man's words,
'I have nothing at all to say.'

Here's a poem that's surely based on experience. O. Henry is the pseudonym of William Sydney Porter (1862–1910), who left school at 15, worked in a drug store, then on Texas ranches and banks. In 1894 he started *The Rolling Stone*, a humorous weekly. When it failed he joined the *Houston Post* as a reporter and columnist. Around the same time cash was found to have gone missing at a bank in Austin where he had worked. When called to stand trial, he fled to Honduras, staying there until some years later he learned his wife was dying, so returned to look after his family. He was charged, found guilty and sent to prison where he stayed for three years. While there, he started writing short stories in order to earn enough to support his daughter. After his release, he became famous throughout the English speaking world for his entertaining and ingenious short stories.

One – *Calloway's Code* – for which alas there is no room here, takes place in the early twentieth century at the time of the Russian/ Japanese war. Calloway is a young journalist who sends a vitally important message relating to details about the planned Yalu River battle. The Japanese are censoring every message and only two get through. One is from a British reporter, but he has all his information wrong ('from beginning to end' writes O. Henry), so the censor grins and lets it go through.

Calloway gets his message through because it appears harmless – the opening words are *Foregone preconcerted rash witching goes muffled . . .* Everyone in the New York paper is mystified. The paper has no codes that any staff know of and no one can work out what the message means.

One person suggests it needs an 'inverted alphabet cipher' where, for example, the 'r' means 'e'. This is tried rapidly for two minutes but the first word reads: 'Scejtzez', so it's goodbye to that. Someone else asks the oldest member to help just in case he remembers anything.

At that point, Vesey, the youngest reporter, walks in. He has a 32 inch chest and wears a number 14 collar; but his bright Scotch plaid suit gives him presence and confers no obscurity upon his whereabouts. He wears his hat in such a position that people follow him about to see him take it off, convinced that it must be hung upon a peg driven into the back of his head.

After exactly 15 minutes he returns. 'I felt the swing as soon as I saw it,' he says. 'It's simply newspaper English. Old Calloway gives us the cue word, and we use the word that naturally follows it.' Foregone = conclusion. Preconcerted = arrangement. Rash = act. Witching = hour of midnight. Goes = without saying.

So the message is deciphered and the first sentence reads: 'Concluded arrangement to act at hour of midnight without saying', i.e., the battle will start at midnight. Calloway and the paper have a world scoop. Vesey gets a pay rise.

Appendix 4
Frank Sinatra has a cold

The feature *Frank Sinatra Has a Cold* by Gay Talese is one of the most famous pieces of American magazine journalism, often considered not only the greatest profile ever written about Frank Sinatra but one of the greatest profiles ever written. On *Esquire* magazine's 70th anniversary (October 2003) it was named the 'Best Story *Esquire* Ever Published'. It's also one of the most famous profiles ever written without interviewing the subject.

Talese had worked for the *New York Times* for 10 years and felt restricted, so signed a one-year-and-six-story contract with *Esquire*. His first assignment was a profile of Frank Sinatra, difficult because Sinatra had rejected interview requests from *Esquire* for years. Again, Sinatra refused to be interviewed.

Rather than give up, Gay Talese spent three months following Sinatra, observing everything he could and interviewing any members of his entourage who would talk to him. Here are the first three paragraphs, incredibly perceptive, telling and vivid – reporting what he saw. The third paragraph is the most famous.

> Frank Sinatra, holding a glass of bourbon in one hand and a cigarette in the other, stood in a dark corner of the bar between two attractive but fading blondes who sat waiting for him to say something. But he said nothing; he had been silent during much of the evening, except now in this private club in Beverly Hills he seemed even more distant, staring out through the smoke and semidarkness into a large room beyond the bar where dozens of young couples sat huddled around small tables or twisted in the center of the floor to the clamorous clang of folk-rock music blaring from the stereo. The two blondes knew, as

did Sinatra's four male friends who stood nearby, that it was a bad idea to force conversation upon him when he was in this mood of sullen silence, a mood that had hardly been uncommon during this first week of November, a month before his fiftieth birthday.

Sinatra had been working in a film that he now disliked, could not wait to finish; he was tired of all the publicity attached to his dating the twenty-year-old Mia Farrow, who was not in sight tonight; he was angry that a CBS television documentary of his life, to be shown in two weeks, was reportedly prying into his privacy, even speculating on his possible friendship with Mafia leaders; he was worried about his starring role in an hour-long NBC show entitled *Sinatra – A Man and His Music*, which would require that he sing eighteen songs with a voice that at this particular moment, just a few nights before the taping was to begin, was weak and sore and uncertain. Sinatra was ill. He was the victim of an ailment so common that most people would consider it trivial. But when it gets to Sinatra it can plunge him into a state of anguish, deep depression, panic, even rage. Frank Sinatra had a cold.

Sinatra with a cold is Picasso without paint, Ferrari without fuel – only worse. For the common cold robs Sinatra of that uninsurable jewel, his voice, cutting into the core of his confidence, and it affects not only his own psyche but also seems to cause a kind of psychosomatic nasal drip within dozens of people who work for him, drink with him, love him, depend on him for their own welfare and stability. A Sinatra with a cold can, in a small way, send vibrations through the entertainment industry and beyond as surely as a President of the United States, suddenly sick, can shake the national economy.

The rest of the profile can be read on *Esquire*'s website (www.esquire.com/features/esq1003-oct_sinatra_rev_).

Appendix 5
One way to get out of prison

Here's a great example of how valuable quick thinking can be – especially for those who go round the world asking questions. It's by Virginia Waite, then writing for the *Daily Telegraph*.

> . . . I was arrested by the Ugandan army and accused of being a spy because I was carrying maps of Tanzania, Rwanda and Zaire, useful for my travel writing and research for a book I had been commissioned to write. This was in 1972, when President Amin was throwing out the Asians.
>
> The journey to jail from upcountry Fort Portal had been 200 miles of winding narrow dirt track through remote hills, jungle scenery and occasional banana plantations. There had been many road-blocks under the 'control' of stoned, drunken quasi-soldiers. The police at Entebbe declined to lock me up in either of the two cells, crammed and stinking with prisoners. Instead I lay down on a bench in the office, which was where a drunken Ugandan soldier found me in the early hours of the morning. He was swearing and threatening and I countered with the only words in Swahili I knew: 'Jambo, wapi simba?' ('Hello, where are the lions?') He was so astounded at these unexpected words from an unexpected white woman that he retreated fast.
>
> The police station was bereft of all facilities, including water, so they 'compensated' by sending across to Lake Victoria Hotel on the nearby lakeside for breakfast to be delivered. Astonishingly, a waiter turned up bearing a silver tray upon which reposed a teapot, cup, milk, toast and butter. 'Is it cash or will you sign for it?' he asked. I paid cash and on the back of the bill scribbled a note to the British High Commission in Kampala telling them my whereabouts. Even more astonishingly, this message got through.

Disappointingly, police custody did not last long and the army once more picked me up and took me to their barracks in Kampala where prisoners, arms roped behind their backs, were being dragged past with whiplash marks on their naked torsos. I talked and talked until the army decided to be rid of me. Back at my hotel, my room had been ransacked. I crammed what remained into a suitcase and was then driven, with no explanation, to Entebbe airport for 'official' deportation. And, yes, I was very glad to leave.

Appendix 6
The journalist and the Queen

Some interviews are impossible. Andrew Pierce – assistant editor of the *Daily Telegraph* – was in a line-up at a charity reception in St James's Palace years back and to his astonishment the Queen paused in front of him, said hello and asked 'What do you do?' Here's his story, recounted in *The Week* (17 November 2007).

> He blushed and stammered 'You can't speak to me.'
>
> 'But I can,' she replied.
>
> 'I'm sure you can't,' said Pierce.
>
> 'But I'm the Queen,' she trilled with a broad smile. 'So, who are you?'
>
> Pierce spluttered that he was a journalist and had been told by the organisers that the Queen never spoke to the press. 'Who do you work for?' she persisted. *The Times*, he said.
>
> 'Ah,' she said, smiling even more broadly. 'Rupert Murdoch. You're quite right. I can't talk to you.'

Appendix 7
Not the way to get promoted

Doctors bury their mistakes, journalists put theirs on the front page.

Old saying

CORRECTION

The map of Europe, Northern Africa and the Arab nations published in Monday's editions contains the following errors: Libya was labeled as the Ukraine; Bulgaria and Romania were transposed; Bosnia-Herzegovina was identified as Bosnia; Montenegro should have been identified as a separate state bordering Serbia; Cyprus and the West Bank were not labeled; Andorra, a country between France and Spain, was not labeled; the Crimean Peninsula appeared twice on the Black Sea; Kuwait was not identified by name, instead the initials of the Knight-Ridder News Service were in its place. The map was supplied by Knight-Ridder and labeled by a Virginian-Pilot staff artist.

From the *Columbia Journalism Review* in a section named 'The Lower case' – credited to *The Virginian-Pilot* (Virginia Beach, Va.; 24 November 1992)

Glossary

Journalism is rich in jargon. Some of it comes from printing (*book* for magazine); or survives from the pre-computer age (*spike* for rejected copy); or is imported from the United States (*clippings* for cuttings). It is often punchy and graphic (*ambush*, *bust*, *fireman*). But if it crops up in copy (e.g. in stories about the media) the sub will usually have to change it (replace 'story' by 'report') or explain it (after 'chapel' insert 'office branch' in brackets). The obvious exception is in publications for journalists such as *Press Gazette* and the *Journalist*.

ABC: Audit Bureau of Circulations – source of independently verified circulation figures
ad: advertisement
add: extra copy to add to existing story
advance: 1 text of speech or statement issued to journalists beforehand; 2 expenses paid before a trip
advertorial: presented as by editorial agencies (*see* news agencies, e.g. PA and Reuters)
agony column: regular advice given on personal problems sent in by readers; hence agony aunt
ambush: journalists lying in wait for unsuspecting, unwilling interviewee
ampersand: symbol for 'and'
angle: particular approach to story, journalist's point of view in writing it
art editor: visual journalist responsible for design and layout of publication
artwork: illustrations (e.g. drawings, photographs) prepared for reproduction
ascender: the part of a lower-case letter (e.g. b and d) that sticks out above the x-height in a typeface
attribution: identifying the journalist's source of information or quote
author's (corrections, marks): proof corrections by writer of story

back number, issue: previous issue of publication
back of the book: second part of magazine (after the centre spread)
backbench, the: senior newspaper journalists who make key production decisions
backgrounder: explanatory feature to accompany news story
bad break: clumsy hyphenation at the end of a line
banner (headline): one in large type across front page
basket: where copy goes – once a physical basket, now a digital folder
bastard measure: typeset to a width that is not standard for the page
beard: the space between a letter and the edge of the base on which it is designed
beat: American term for specialist area covered by reporter
bill(board): poster promoting edition of newspaper, usually highlighting main news story
black: duplicate of written story (from colour of carbon paper once used with typewriter)
bleed: (of an image) go beyond the type area to the edge of a page
blob par: extra paragraph introduced by blob
blob: solid black circle used for display effect or to tabulate lists
blog: short for 'web log', is an online diary or journal. Is also used as a verb: 'to blog'
blow up: enlarge (part of) photograph blown quote (*see* pull quote)
blurb: displayed material promoting contents of another page or future issue
body copy: the main text of a story, as opposed to page furniture
body type: the main typeface in which a story is set (as opposed to display)
bold: thick black type, used for emphasis
book: printer's (and so production journalist's) term for magazine
bot: black on tone
box: copy enclosed by rules to give it emphasis and/or separate it from the main text
breaker: typographical device, for example crosshead, used to break up text on the page
brief: 1 short news item; 2 instruction to journalist on how to approach story
bring up: bring forward part of story to earlier position
broadsheet: large-format newspaper
bromide: photographic print
bullet (point): another term for blob
bureau: office of news agency or newspaper office in foreign country

business-to-business: current term for what were once called 'trade' magazines, that is, those covering a business area, profession, craft or trade
bust: (of a headline) be too long for the space available
buy-up interview: exclusive bought by publication
byline: writer's name as it appears in print at the beginning of a story

c & lc: capital and lower-case letters
call out: another term for pull quote
calls (also check calls): routine phone calls made by reporters to organisations such as police and fire brigade to see if a story is breaking
camera-ready: (e.g. artwork) prepared for reproduction
caps: capital letters
caption: words used with a picture (usually underneath), identifying where necessary and relating it to the accompanying story
caption story: extension of picture caption into a self-contained story
cast off: estimate amount of printed matter copy would make
casual: journalist employed by the shift
catch(line): short word (not printed) identifying different elements of a story in the editorial process
centre: set type with equal space on either side
centre spread: middle opening of tabloid or magazine
chapel: office branch of media union (the shop steward is the father, FoC, or mother, MoC, of the chapel)
character: unit of measurement for type including letters, figures, punctuation marks and spaces
chequebook journalism: paying large sums for stories
chief sub: senior subeditor in charge of the others
city desk: financial section of British national newspaper (in the United States the city desk covers home news)
classified advertising: small ads 'classified' by subject matter, grouped in a separate section
clippings/clips: American term for cuttings
close quotes: end of section in direct quotes
close up: reduce space between lines, words or characters
CMYK: cyan, magenta, yellow and black, the process (basic printing) colours
col: column
colour piece: news story written as feature with emphasis on journalist's reactions
colour sep(aration)s: method by which the four process colours (CMYK) are separated from a colour original
column: 1 standard vertical division of page; 2 regular feature by journalist often encouraged to be opinionated and/or entertaining
column rule: light rule between columns of type

conference: meeting of editorial staff to plan current/next issue
consumer magazines: the category includes specialist titles (e.g. *Angling Times*), women's magazines and those of general interest
contact sheet: photographer's sheet of small prints
contacts book: a journalist's list of contacts with details of phone, fax, email, etc.
contents bill: *see* bill
controlled circulation: free distribution of specialist title to target readership by geography (free newspapers) or interest group (business-to-business magazines)
copy: text of story
copy taster: *see* taster
copyright: right to reproduce original material
copytaker: telephone typist who takes down copy from reporter
corr: correspondent
correction: published statement correcting errors in story
correspondent: journalist covering specialist area, for example education
coverlines: selling copy on front cover
credit (line): name of photographer or illustrator as it appears in print next to their work
Cromalins: the Dupont system of glossy colour proofs
crop: cut (image) to size or for better effect
crosshead: line or lines, taken from the text, set bigger and bolder than the body type and inserted between paragraphs to liven up page
cut: shorten or delete copy
cut-out: illustration with background masked, painted or cut to make it stand out on the page
cuts: cuttings
cuttings: stories taken (originally cut) from newspapers and filed electronically under subject
cuttings job: story that is over-dependent on cuttings

dateline: place from which copy is filed
deadline: time story (or any part of it) is due
deck: originally one of a series of headlines stacked on top of each other; now usually used to mean one line of a headline
delayed drop: device in news story of delaying important facts for effect
delete: remove
descender: the part of a lower-case letter (e.g. g and j) that sticks out below the x-height in a typeface
desk: newspaper department, for example picture desk
deskman: American term for male subeditor
diary column: gossip column

diary, the: list of news events to be covered; hence an off-diary story is one originated by the reporter
direct input: transmission of copy direct from the journalist's keyboard to the computer for typesetting (as opposed to the old system in which compositors retyped copy)
disclaimer: statement explaining that a particular person or organisation was not the subject of a previously published story
display ads: ordinary (not 'classified') ads which appear throughout a publication
display type: type for headlines etc.
district reporter: one covering a particular area away from the main office
doorstepping: reporters lying in wait for (usually) celebrities outside their homes
double: a story published twice in the same issue of a publication
double (page) spread: two facing pages in a magazine, whether advertising or editorial
double-column: (of text, headline, illustration) across two columns
download: to transfer material from the internet onto your own computer
downtable subs: those other than the chief sub and deputies
drop cap, letter: outsize initial capital letter used to start story or section; it drops down alongside the text which is indented to accommodate it
drop quotes: outsize quotes used to mark quoted matter
dummy: 1 pre-publication edition of new publication used to sell advertising and experiment editorially; 2 blank version of publication, for example to show quality and weight of paper; 3 complete set of page proofs

edition: version of newspaper printed for particular circulation area or time
editor: senior journalist responsible for publication or section
editor's conference: main planning meeting for next issue
editorial: 1 leading article expressing editorial opinion; 2 content that is not advertising
em, en: units of measurement for type – the width of the two letters m and n
embargo: time before which an organisation supplying material, for example by press release, does not want it published
ends: the story ends here
EPD: electronic picture desk
EPS file: Encapsulated PostScript file
exclusive: claim by publication that it has a big story nobody else has
exes: journalists' out-of-pocket expenses

face: type design
facing matter: (of advertising) opposite editorial

facsimile: exact reproduction, as with electronic transmission of pages
feature: article that goes beyond reporting of facts to explain and/or entertain; also used of any editorial material that is not news or listings; hence feature writer, features editor
file: transmit copy
filler: short news item to fill space
fireman: traditional term for reporter sent to trouble spot when story breaks
fit: (of copy etc.) to occupy exactly the space available
flannel panel: magazine's address, contact information and list of staff
flash: brief urgent message from news agency
flatplan: page-by-page plan of issue
flip: (of picture) transpose left to right
flush left or right: (of type) having one consistent margin with the other ragged
fold, the: centre fold in a newspaper so that only the upper half of the paper ('above the fold') is visible at the point of sale
folio: page (number)
follow up: take published story as the starting point for an update
format: 1 size, shape or style of publication or section; 2 computer instruction; hence to format
fount (pronounced font and now often spelt that way): typeface
free(sheet): free newspaper
freebie: something useful or pleasant, often a trip, supplied free to journalists
freelance: self-employed journalist who sells material to various outlets
freelancer: American term for freelance
fudge: another term for stop press
full out: (of type) not indented

galley proof: typeset proof not yet made up into a page
gatefold: an extra page which folds out from a magazine
ghost writer: journalist writing on behalf of someone else, often by interviewing them; hence to ghost (e.g. a column)
gone to bed: passed for press so too late for corrections
grams per square metre (gsm; g/m2): the measure used to define the weight of paper
graphics: visual material, usually drawn
grid: design skeleton specifying (e.g.) number and width of columns
gutter: space between two facing pages; can also be used of space between columns

H & J: (of copy on screen) hyphenated and justified, so in the form in which it will be typeset

hack, hackette: jocular terms for journalist
hair space: thinnest space between typeset letters
half-tone: illustration broken into dots of varying sizes
hand-out: printed material, for example press release, distributed to journalists
hanging indent: copy set with first line of each paragraph full out and subsequent ones indented
hard copy: copy on paper, for example printout, rather than screen
head, heading: headline
heavy: broadsheet newspaper
heavy type: thicker than standard
hold (over): keep material for future use
hot metal: old typesetting system in which type was cast from molten metal
house ad: publisher's advertisement in its own publication
house journal: publication for employees of a particular organisation
house style: the way a publication chooses to publish in matters of detail

IM or instant messaging: a method to connect to another computer via the internet. What is typed on the first computer can be read on the second one and so an online 'conversation' takes place
imposition: arrangement of pages for printing
imprint: name and address of publisher and printer
in pro: in proportion (used of visual material to be reduced)
indent: set copy several characters in from left-hand margin
in-house: inside a media organisation
input: type copy into computer
insert: 1 extra copy to be included in existing story; 2 printed matter inserted in publication after printing and binding
intro: first paragraph of story; also used (confusingly) in some magazine offices to mean standfirst
ISDN: integrated services digital network – a means of transmitting editorial material between offices, to printers, etc.
italics: italic (sloping) type

jack-line: another word for widow
journo: jocular term for journalist
justified: typeset with consistent margins

kern: reduce the space between characters in typeset copy
kicker: introductory part of caption or headline

kill: drop a story; hence kill fee for freelance whose commissioned story is not used
knocking copy: story written with negative angle

label: (of headline) without a verb
landscape: horizontal picture
layout: arrangement of body type, headlines etc. and illustrations on the page
lead: 1 main story on a page; 2 tip-off or idea for story (in the United States the intro of a story is called the lead)
leader: leading article expressing editorial opinion
leader dots: three dots used to punctuate
leading (pronounced 'ledding'): space between lines (originally made by inserting blank slugs of lead between lines of type)
leg: column of typeset copy
legal: send material to be checked for legal problems, for example libel
legal kill: lawyer's instruction not to use
lensman: American term for male photographer
letter spacing: space between letters
libel: defamatory statement in permanent or broadcast form
lift: 1 use all or most of a story taken from one newspaper edition in the next; 2 steal a story from another media outlet and reproduce it with few changes
ligature: two or more joined letters
light face: type lighter than standard
linage (this spelling preferred to lineage): payment to freelances by the line; also refers to classified advertising without illustration
line drawing: drawing made up of black strokes
listings: lists of entertainment and other events with basic details
literal: typographical error
lobby, the: specialist group of political reporters covering parliament
local corr: local correspondent
logo: name, title or recognition word in particular design used on regular section or column; also used of magazine's front-page title
lower case: ordinary letters (not caps)

make-up: assembly of type and illustrations on the page ready for reproduction
mark up: specify the typeface, size and width in which copy is to be set
masking: covering part of photograph for reproduction
masthead: publication's front-page title
measure: width of typesetting

medium type: between light and heavy
merchandising: details of stockists and prices in consumer features
mf: more copy follows
model release: contract signed by photographic model authorising use of pictures
mono(chrome): printed in one colour, usually black
more: more copy follows
mug shot: photograph showing head (and sometimes shoulders)
must: copy that must appear, for example apology or correction
mutton: old name for an em

neg: photographic negative
news agency: supplier of news and features to media outlets
news desk: organising centre of newsroom
newsman: American term for male reporter
newsprint: standard paper on which newspapers are printed
newsroom: news reporters' room
nib: news in brief – short news item
night lawyer: barrister who reads newspaper proofs for legal problems
nose: intro of story; hence to renose – rewrite intro
NUJ: National Union of Journalists
nut: old name for an en; hence nutted, type indented one en

obit: obituary
off-diary: *see* diary, the
off-the-record: statements made to a journalist on the understanding that they will not be reported directly or attributed
on spec: uncommissioned (material submitted by freelance)
online: to be on the internet – an online interview is one published on the internet as opposed to in traditional print format
on-the-record: statements made to a journalist that can be reported and attributed
op-ed: feature page facing page with leading articles
open quotes: start of section in direct quotes
originals: photographs or other visual material for reproduction
orphan: first line of a paragraph at the foot of a page or column
out take: another term for pull quote
overlay: sheet of transparent paper laid over artwork with instructions on how to process it
overline: another word for strapline
overmatter: typeset material that does not fit the layout and must be cut
overprint: print over a previously printed background

PA: Press Association, Britain's national news agency
package: main feature plus sidebars
page furniture: displayed type, for example headlines, standfirsts and captions, used to project copy
page plan: editorial instructions for layout
page proof: proof of a made-up page
pagination: the number of pages in a publication; also a newspaper system's ability to make up pages
panel: another word for box
paparazzo/i: photographer(s) specialising in pursuing celebrities
par, para: paragraph
paste-up: page layout pasted into position
patch: specialist area covered by reporter
pay-off: final twist or flourish in the last paragraph of a story
peg: reason for publishing feature at a particular time
photomontage: illustration created by combining several photographs
pic, pix: press photograph(s)
pica: unit of type measurement
pick-up (of photographs): those that already exist and can therefore be picked up by journalists covering a story
picture desk: organising centre of collection and editing of pictures
piece: article
plate: printing image carrier from which pages are printed
podcast: a digital sound or video file distributed over the internet that can be played on an iPod, MP3 player or other suitable equipment. Also used as a verb 'to podcast'
point: 1 full stop; 2 standard unit of type size
pool: group of reporters sharing information and releasing it to other media organisations
PostScript: Adobe's page description language
PR(O): public relations (officer); hence someone performing a public relations role
press cuttings: *see* cuttings
press release: written announcement or promotional material by organisation sent to media outlets and individual journalists
profile: portrait in words of individual or organisation
proof: printout of part or whole of page so it can be checked and corrected
proofread: check proofs; hence proofreader
publisher: 1 publishing company; 2 individual in magazine publishing company with overall responsibility for title or group of titles
puff: story promoting person or organisation
pull: proof; to pull is to take a proof

pull (out) quote (blown quote, call out, out take): short extract from text set in larger type as part of page layout
pullout: separate section of publication that can be pulled out
pyramid: (usually inverted) conventional structure for news story with most important facts in intro

query: question mark
queue: collection of stories held in a computer
quote: verbatim quotation
quotes: quotation marks

ragged: (of type) with uneven margin
raised cap: outsize initial capital letter used to start story or section; it is raised above the text
range left or right: (of type) have one consistent margin with the other ragged
register: alignment of coloured inks on the printed page
rejig: rewrite copy, particularly in the light of later information
renose: rewrite intro of a story
reporter: gatherer and writer of news
repro house: company that processes colour pictures ready for printing
retainer: regular payment to local correspondent or freelance
retouch: alter photograph to emphasise particular feature
Reuters: international news agency
reverse indent: another term for hanging indent
reversed out: (type) printed in white on black or tinted background
revise: extra proof to check that corrections have been made
rewrite: write new version of story or section as opposed to subbing on copy
ring-round: story based on series of phone calls
river: white space running down a column of type, caused by space between words
roman: plain upright type
rough: sketch for layout
round-up: gathering of disparate elements for single story
RSI: repetitive strain injury, attributed to overuse and misuse of computer keyboard, mouse, etc.
rule: line between columns or round illustrations
run: period of printing an edition or number of copies printed
run on: (of type) continue from one line, column or page to the next
running foot: title and issue date at the foot of the page
running head: title and issue date at the top of the page
running story: one that is constantly developing, over a newspaper's different editions or a number of days

running turns: pages with no paragraph breaks on first and last lines; also used of columns
rush: second most urgent message from news agency (after flash)

s/s: same size
sans (serif): plain type (*see* serif) – this is an example
scaling (of pictures): calculating depth
schedule: 1 list of jobs for (e.g.) reporters; 2 publication's printing programme
scheme: make a plan of page layout
scoop: jocular word for exclusive
screamer: exclamation mark
screen: the number of dots per square inch of a half-tone
section: 1 separately folded part of newspaper; 2 complete printed sheet making up part of magazine
sell: another word for standfirst, often used in women's magazines
serif: decorative addition to type – this is an example
set and hold: typeset and keep for use later
setting: copy set in type
shift: daily stint worked by staff journalists and casuals
shoot: a photographic session
shy: (of headline) too short for the space available
sidebar: subsidiary story or other material placed next to main story, usually in box
sidehead: subsidiary heading, set flush left
sign-off: writer's name as it appears in print at the end of a story
sketch: light-hearted account of events, especially parliamentary
slip: newspaper edition for particular area or event
small caps: capital letters in smaller size of the same typeface
snap: early summary by news agency of important story to come
snapper: jocular term for press photographer
snaps: press photographs
solid: (of type) set without extra leading
sound bite: a very short piece of a speech taken from a longer speech or an interview which is considered to be the most important point
spike: where rejected copy goes (originally a metal spike)
splash: newspaper's main front-page story
splash sub: subeditor responsible for tabloid's front page
spoiler: attempt by newspaper to reduce impact of rival's exclusive by publishing similar story
spot colour: second colour (after black) used in printing publication
spread: two facing pages
standfirst: introductory matter accompanying headline, particularly used in features

stet: ignore deletion or correction (Latin for 'let it stand')
stone: bench where pages were made up; hence stone sub – subeditor who makes final corrections and cuts on page proofs
stop press: small area on back page of newspaper left blank for late news in days of hot metal
story: article, especially news report
strap(line): subsidiary headline above main headline
Street, the: Fleet Street, where many newspapers once had their offices
stringer: local correspondent; freelance on contract to a news organisation
style: house style
style book/style sheet: where house style is recorded
sub: subeditor
subhead: subsidiary headline
subtitle: another word for standfirst

tab(loid): popular small-format newspaper such as the *Sun*
tagline: explanatory note under headline
take: section of copy for setting
take back: (on proof) take words back to previous line
take over: (on proof) take words forward to next line
taster: production journalist who checks and selects copy; also coverline
think piece: feature written to show and provoke thought
tie-in: story connected with the one next to it
tint: shaded area on which type can be printed
tip(-off): information supplied (and usually paid for) whether by freelance or member of the public
titlepiece: traditional term for name of magazine as it appears on the cover – now replaced by masthead and logo
TOT: triumph over tragedy, feature formula particularly popular in women's magazines
tracking: space between characters
trade names: product names (e.g. Hoover, Kleenex, Velcro)
tranny: transparency – photograph in film form
trans(pose): reverse order
turn: part of story continued on a later page
typeface: a complete range of type in a particular style, for example Times New Roman
typescale: measuring rule for type
typo: American term for typographical error
typography: craft of using type

u/lc: upper and lower case
underscore: underline

unj(ustified): text set flush left, ragged right
upload: to transfer material from your own computer onto the internet
upper and lower case: mixture of capitals and ordinary letters
upper case: capital letters

vignette: illustration whose edges gradually fade to nothing
vodcast: a video podcast
vox pop: series of street interviews (Latin: *vox populi* – voice of the people)

weight: thickness or boldness of letters in a typeface
white space: area on page with no type or illustration
widow: single word or part of word at the end of a paragraph on a line by itself; originally the last line of a paragraph at the top of a page or column
wire: a means of transmitting copy by electronic signal; hence wire room
wob: white on black – type reversed out
wot: white on tone

x-height: height of the lower-case letters of a typeface (excluding ascenders and descenders)

Recommended books and films

Interview collections

The two books by Lynn Barber include some of her finest interviews, together with excellent advice in the outstanding introductions. American John Brady's book is very old (try Amazon) but crammed with wisdom.

Barber, Lynn, *Mostly Men*, Viking, 1991
—— *Demon Barber*, Viking, 1998
Brady, John, *The Craft of Interviewing*, Vintage, 1977
Davies, Hunter, *Hunting People: Thirty Years of Interviews with the Famous*, Mainstream Publishing, 1994
Gill, A A, *Previous Convictions*, Phoenix, 2006
Silvester, Christopher (ed.), *The Penguin Book of Interviews*, Viking, 1993
Terkel, Studs, *Working*, Penguin, 1985

General

Alvarez, Al, *Where Did it All Go Right?*, Richard Cohen Books, 1999
Davies, Nick, *Flat Earth News*, Chatto & Windus, 2008
Grobel, Lawrence, *The Art of Interview: Lessons from a Master of the Craft*, Three Rivers Press, 2004
Knightley, Phillip, *A Hack's Progress*, Viking, 1997
Lee-Potter, Emma, *Moving On*, Judy Piatkus, 2000
Marr, Andrew, *My Trade*, Macmillan, 2004
Simpson, John, *Strange Places, Questionable People*, Macmillan, 1998
Watkins, Alan, *A Short Walk Down Fleet Street*, Duckworth, 2000
Wolfe, Tom, and Johnson, E W (eds), *The New Journalism*, Picador, 1990

Body language and gestures

Axtell, Roger E, *Gestures: the DO'S and TABOOS of Body Language Around the World*, John Wiley & Sons, 1997

Comer, Michael and Stephen, Timothy, *Deception at Work*, Gower, 2004
Ekman, Paul, *Emotions Revealed: Understanding Faces and Feelings*, Orion, 2004
Pease, Allan and Pease, Barbara, *The Definitive Book of Body Language*, Orion, 2004

Investigative journalism

Two great books.

The Liar, subtitled *The Fall of Jonathan Aitken*, by Luke Harding, Davie Leigh and David Palister (Penguin, 1997), is as dramatic as Aitken's life and the court case in which he sued the *Guardian*. The vital evidence arrived just in time to exonerate the paper. An inspiring tale, dramatically and vividly told.

Selling Hitler by Robert Harris (Penguin, 1986) tells the story of how Rupert Murdoch's *Times* and *Sunday Times* top staff were duped into buying the reprint rights of a phoney diary, supposedly Hitler's – all because the right people weren't asked the right questions. Riveting and valuable.

Insight into politics

Anonymous (now known to be Joe Klein), *Primary Colors*, Vintage, 1996
Dobbs, Michael, *House of Cards*, Collins, 1989
Jones, N, *Soundbites and Spin Doctors: How Politicians Manipulate the Media – and Vice Versa*, Cassell, 1995
Stephanopoulos, George, *All Too Human*, Hutchinson, 1999

Techniques

Berne, Eric, *What Do You Say After You Say Hello?*, 2nd edition, Andre Deutsch, 2003 (obtainable from STC, 17 Grove Lane, London SE5 8RD; tel. 020 7703 5400)
Markham, Ursula, *How to Deal with Difficult People*, Thorsons, 1993

Law and ethics

Keeble, Richard, *Ethics for Journalists*, Routledge, 2001
Mason, Peter, and Smith, Derrick, *Magazine Law*, Routledge, 1998
Welsh, Tom, Greenwood, Walter, and Banks, David, *McNae's Essential Law for Journalists*, 19th edition, Oxford University Press, 2007

Old but worth reading

Try Amazon.

Day, Robin, *Grand Inquisitor*, Weidenfeld & Nicholson, 1989
Mitford, Jessica, *The Making of a Muckraker*, Quartet, 1980

Movies

Well worth viewing:

'The Paper' (Universal, 1994; dir: Ron Howard) Michael Keaton, Glenn Close, Robert Duvall. A hectic 24 hours on a tabloid New York paper. Chaos reigns as the staff get the issue out. Cynical, recognisable, funny, excellent performances.

'Wag the Dog' (Baltimore Pictures, 1997; dir: Barry Levinson) Dustin Hoffman, Robert De Niro, Woody Harrelson. Two weeks before the US presidential election a White House adviser creates a phoney war to divert voters' attention from the president's scandalous behaviour. Cynical and worryingly funny.

Index